A MANAGER'S GUIDE TO SELF-DEVELOPMENT
Third Edition

Mike Pedler
John Burgoyne
Tom Boydell

McGRAW-HILL BOOK COMPANY

London · New York · St Louis · San Francisco · Auckland · Bogotá
Caracas · Lisbon · Madrid · Mexico · Milan · Montreal · New Delhi
Panama · Paris · San Juan · São Paulo · Singapore · Sydney · Tokyo · Toronto

Published by
McGRAW-HILL Book Company Europe
Shoppenhangers Road, Maidstone, Berkshire, SL6 2QL, England
Telephone 01628 23432
Fax 01628 770224

British Library Cataloguing in Publication Data

Pedler, Mike
   Manager's Guide to Self-development. –
3 Rev.ed.
  I. Title
  658.409

  ISBN 0-07-707829-2

Library of Congress Cataloging-in-Publication Data

Pedler, Mike.
   A manager's guide to self-development / Mike Pedler, John Burgoyne,
Tom Boydell.—3rd ed.
     p.   cm.
   Includes bibliographical references and index.
   ISBN 0-07-707829-2
   1. Management. I. Burgoyne, John (John G.) II. Boydell, Tom.
III. Title.
HD31.P36 1994
658.4'09—dc20
                                                   94-18933
                                                    CIP

34 CL 9654

Typeset by Paston Press Ltd, Loddon, Norfolk
and printed and bound in Great Britain by Clays Ltd, St Ives plc

Contents

Acknowledgements

Our thanks to the many people who have contributed to this book; who taught us and from whom we have borrowed. Especial thanks to Tina Pedler who, in 1985, toothcombed the first edition and took out the sexism, ethnocentricism and sundry other embarrassments; and to Reg Walker and Jacinta Elliot who, in 1993, undertook a critical reading of the second edition, drafted five of the new activities and made many helpful suggestions for new references.

Introduction

1 The philosophy of the book

This book, which is an aid to management self-development rather than a repository of wisdom, is based on a simple fundamental premise:

> that any effective system for management development must increase the manager's capacity and willingness to take control over, and responsibility for, events—particularly for themselves and their own learning.

While this is not a new concept it is one which is far from recognized in our current society and by management in general.

Most of us, if asked to think about how we have learned, think of our experiences when attempts have been made to *teach* us.[1] If, on the other hand, we are asked about *problems we have solved* we think about difficult situations we have faced and managed to overcome. However, in solving problems we don't just deal with the immediate difficulty, we discover a solution which we can use again in some form, *and* we may also become better at solving problems generally. Problem solving *is*, to a large extent, *learning*.

In the managerial world, dealing with live problems, rather than being taught, is the major source of significant learning. When it comes to a 'crunch' decision, for example selecting a new senior manager, what really matters is track record—whether the person has dealt successfully with a number of difficult situations. Information on what has been *taught*, through involvement on formal management development programmes, does not usually carry much weight.

The implication for the ambitious is clear: *get a slice of the action, deal with it in a way that is clearly successful, and be seen to have done it* (the visibility factor).

Changing organizations

However, today's managers have to be more than ambitious in simple career terms. We are emerging from an era when success for

3

most managers meant climbing higher and higher on the organizational climbing frame, with the occasional bold leap across to an even higher level on an adjacent structure.

Throughout the 1980s and 1990s we have seen many of these climbing frames collapse, break up or shrink, and become 'leaner' and 'flatter'. The grim experience of many managers has been of throwing each other off the frame to make room for the survivors, who get used to sideways moves and increased responsibilities. In the light of this reality, just having a job has become more prized, and sideways moves can be found to offer variety and development opportunities.

Above all, there is a realization that success and satisfaction does not come from 'possessing' a large chunk of managerial territory in an invulnerable blue chip company, but from being part of a well run and effective organization which knows what it is doing, where it is going and what part each person's unique contribution can make. This has perhaps been the key significance of the 'Excellence' movement of the 1980s,[2] the Total Quality movement[3] and, more recently, the 'Learning Company' idea.[4] People want to work in organizations which they believe are good, which know why they are good and know how they can stay this way.

This adds up to everyone exercising a greater degree of *self-management*, aligning their efforts with others through allegiance to corporate values and missions, rather than via the external regulation of job descriptions, management by objectives and hierarchical supervision. Information technology is speeding up this trend and distributing knowledge and awareness to make possible more self-responsible working, while sharpening the remaining need for supervision by taking away routine information collection and processing. This leads to a new definition of management in the 1990s.

Learning on behalf of the organization

The manager's job is to learn on behalf of the organization. Operating systems are increasingly self-regulating, and the manager's contribution is focused on how these can be improved (*incremental organizational learning*) or working out what the next generation of systems should be and working towards those (*discontinuous organizational learning*).

An organization which encourages and develops these qualities in its people can be called a Learning Company—literally a group of people who learn in company, not only as individuals, but also as a whole organism.

This book is based on a framework of qualities, skills and competencies for management self-development. These qualities are concerned with a proactive, self-managed and self-developmental approach to being a manager. The Learning Company *requires* its people to manage themselves and to learn for themselves, their colleagues and for the company as a whole.

Formal management development as deskilling

Perhaps the reason why formal management development has not really made it as a significant force is that it has, unintentionally, *deskilled* people. Why is this? The explanation may lie in Marshall McLuhan's 1960s adage: *the medium is the message.*

The *message* from formal management development is concerned with leadership skills, project management, corporate strategy and so on, but what is the *medium* doing? The messages coming from the medium are, we suggest:

> There is an expert for every type of management problem; don't try to solve it on your own—call in the experts.

> You don't know how to learn? Don't worry, you don't need to. We're here to manage that for you. If you need a 're-tread', don't try to do it yourself, come back to us.

Such messages *deskill* people. This book provides a vehicle for *self-development* based on the premise that effective management development must increase a manager's capacity and willingness to take control over, and responsibility for, events.

What is self-development?

Self-development is personal development, with the person taking primary responsibility for her or his own learning and for choosing the means to achieve this. This is a simple answer, for the sake of brevity, to what can be a complex issue. Other views on the meaning and purpose of self-development are:

● career development and advancement;
● improving performance in an existing job;
● developing certain specific qualities and skills;
● achieving total potential—self actualization.

This book will help with all of these, especially the last three. Self-development may well lead to advancement, but our concern is with the development of all the people in the organization and of the organization itself.

Here is an invitation to work on your own personal and professional development, making use of our suggestions on strategy and tactics, and of the resources we have provided as *you* think fit. Go to it.

REFERENCES

1. Kolb, D. A., I. M. Rubin and J. M. McIntyre, *Organizational Psychology: An Experiential Approach*, Prentice-Hall, 5th edn 1990.
2. See, for example, Peters, T. J. and R. H. Waterman, *In Search of Excellence*, Harper & Row, 1982.
3. See, for example, Deming, W. E., *Out of the Crisis*, Cambridge University Press, 1986.
4. Pedler, M. J., J. G. Burgoyne and T. H. Boydell, *The Learning Company: A Strategy for Sustainable Development*, McGraw-Hill, 1991.

2 How the book works

If you are interested in having a go at this self-development programme you will need first to take some time thinking about where
you are now and where you want to be in terms of work and career
activities, in thinking about the skills you have and those you need
to develop, and in working out learning goals and planning a
personal learning programme.

You are likely to have only limited and unpredictable time periods
to carry out the project. This book is designed, therefore, so that
you can work on some of the exercises a bit at a time, using odd half
hours on train journeys, between meetings, in the bath, or in bed if
you are keen enough. Some of the activities need to be tackled at
work, such as observing how meetings work and trying out different
forms of personal intervention. Others you can work through in
informal contact with colleagues, over lunch for instance, to test
their perceptions against your own.

Finally, you face an apparent paradox. If you work on a self-
development project in which *you* take responsibility for deciding
what you need to learn and how to learn it, on what basis are you to
accept help from other sources including, obviously, the authors of
this book? There is no paradox as long as you accept that the book
offers suggestions rather than instructions. It is for you to decide at
each stage whether what we suggest is right for you, and whether
there is a better way that you can think of for yourself. We suggest
(but do not instruct) that you spend time, if you work through parts
of this book, considering whether you can improve on our suggestions *for yourself*. Keep in mind our explanation that the book is a
series of suggestions and that you will only learn if you decide for
yourself whether to follow the suggestions or not. Because it would
be cumbersome to begin every sentence 'we suggest that you
consider . . .' or 'one way to look at this is to consider that . . .',
much of the rest of the book will give straightforward descriptions
of things to do, and make blunt assertions about management,
which may tend to sound like instructions, commands, orders, or

statements of ultimate truth. This is for clarity and brevity. Remember, it is for *you to decide* whether to believe our interpretations of reality or accept our suggestions.

The book is in two parts. The first is designed to help you set learning goals for yourself and to help you plan to achieve these goals. The second is designed to help you carry out that plan.

We suggest that you work through the first part sequentially, using the 'life planning' option incorporated in it, if appropriate. When you reach the end of Part 1 you should have a list of areas in which you recognize the need to develop yourself.

Part 2 consists of a set of resources, in the form of exercises and other suggested activities which you can use to achieve some of your learning goals. Part 1 ends with some general suggestions on how to use the activities, and a guide, in the form of the 'Learning Goal Matrix', which shows which activities might help you achieve which learning goals.

Part 1
Setting and meeting goals for management self-development

As explained in Chapter 2, in this first part of the book we describe some ways of identifying your self-development needs and hence setting goals for yourself.

In fact, there are many ways of doing this, and we have, therefore, had to be selective and choose just two (both of which are shown diagrammatically in the diagram on page 10), thus:

- A career/life-planning exercise (Chapter 3); this takes a relatively large-scale approach, looking at your job and career within the context of your whole life.
- A questionnaire approach (Chapter 5); in fact we give two questionnaires, using different types of response and scoring system. Both are based on a particular model of the qualities of an effective manager, as described in Chapter 4.

Whichever of these you choose (or, of course, you can do them all) you then use the results as the starting point for *domain mapping* (Chapter 3), which helps with setting priorities and goals, and then leads into choosing appropriate activities from Part 2.

These, then, are the formal self-diagnostic activities. However, you will also find that there is an element of diagnosis, as well as action, in many of the subsequent activities in Part 2. Therefore these may also be used, in a different way, as a means of focusing on some of your development needs.

If you would like more reading on the whole process of self-diagnosis, and on some of the pitfalls to avoid, then you will probably find both the following helpful: Tom Boydell's *Management Self-Development: A Guide for Managers, Organisations and Institutions*, published in 1985 by the International Labour Office (ILO) in Geneva, but available from its London Office; and Mike Pedler and Tom Boydell's *Managing Yourself* (Fontana Paperbacks, 1985).

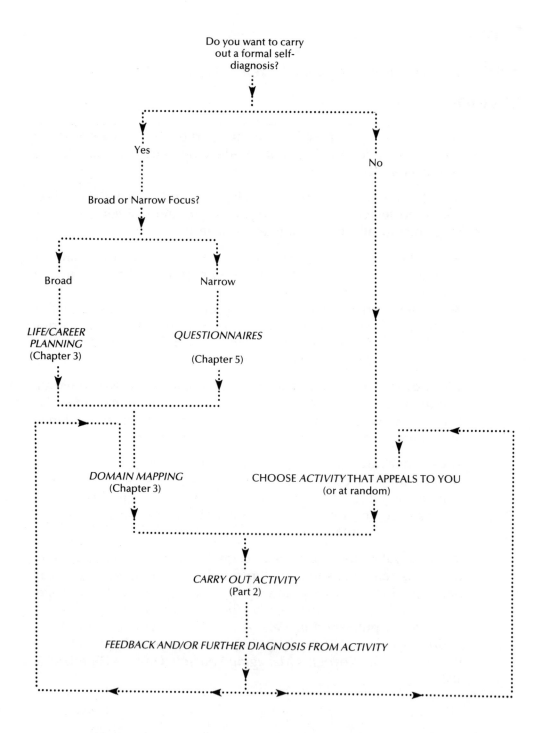

Do you want to carry
out a formal self-
diagnosis?

Yes

No

Broad or Narrow Focus?

Broad

Narrow

*LIFE/CAREER
PLANNING*
(Chapter 3)

QUESTIONNAIRES

(Chapter 5)

DOMAIN MAPPING
(Chapter 3)

CHOOSE *ACTIVITY* THAT APPEALS TO YOU
(or at random)

CARRY OUT ACTIVITY
(Part 2)

FEEDBACK AND/OR FURTHER DIAGNOSIS FROM ACTIVITY

Diagnostic pathway

3 A career/life-planning activity

We are assuming that if you are reading this book you have some interest in a career as a manager, and, as we have just outlined, this chapter takes a relatively broad focus, looking at this career in the context of your life as a whole.

Having said that, there are all sorts of issues that this broad approach can help with. Let's give just a few examples.

- You may be wondering whether or not you want to become a manager.
- You may be wondering whether you could be, either in terms of your abilities and talents, or in terms of creating opportunities for getting into a managerial job.
- On the other hand, you may have been a manager for some time, and are now faced with questions such as: What is my next step?
- Or perhaps you are becoming increasingly aware that something is wrong about the way in which you are balancing (or not!) the demands of being a manager with your domestic and family needs.
- Or again perhaps you have a feeling that something else is missing. OK, you're getting on reasonably well in your job, but so what? What do you *really* want from life? Are you going to achieve it the way things are going?
- Finally, perhaps you are faced with a crisis such as redundancy, illness, separation. What does this mean, not only in terms of loss, but also by way of providing a turning point? How are you handling this?

This short list of examples illustrates one of our fundamental beliefs, namely that it's not possible—and therefore not desirable to try—to separate out our job's and careers from the rest of our lives. They are so much part of each other that it's even a mistake to think of them as 'they'. Rather, better to express it by saying that my job/career/family/relationships/health/spirituality/etc., *is* my life.

For many people the notion of spending time on trying to plan their life may seem a bit odd. However, as the first 'activity' in this book, try this:

How many hours have you spent thinking about and planning:

- your last holiday?
- selecting the house or flat, etc., in which you now live?
- obtaining your hi-fi, video, camera, car, bicycle, or whatever gadget or toy you are addicted to?
- your life?

Can you rank order these in terms first of the amount of time you spent planning them, and then in order of importance?

If, then, you want to spend some time really looking at your life, this activity will be useful.

There are a large number of life-planning exercises available from numerous sources. They tend to differ not only in detail, but also in the extent to which they focus on the past, present, and future. Some are almost entirely past-oriented, although the majority, in contrast, concentrate mainly on the future. The version we give here pays attention to all three—past, present, and future. (We give some sources both of other exercises and broader background material at the end of this chapter.)

You will see that it takes the form of a series of small tasks and questions designed to give you insights into:

- *the past*: events, periods and themes and achievements in your life so far;
- *the present*: issues and questions coming your way, be it a continuation of residue of events, periods and themes from the past; from things that other people in your life are asking you, or telling you; and from events now facing you or on the visible horizon;
- *the future*; determining priorities, choosing from alternative courses of action and taking first steps in implementing your choice.

Obviously, the more you put into the activity, the more you will get out of it. To do it properly will take quite a lot of time, and we suggest that you take it steadily, spreading it out over a few days, tackling a little at a time (perhaps two or three steps each day).

There's no doubt in our mind that the learning and payoff from the activity can be increased if you work with a partner whom you trust and who is interested in working on his or her own life. Or you can do it in a small group, sharing with each other after each step.

The past

Step 1. Events

Look back over your life so far, and write down the main key events, happenings, incidents, turning points that have taken place. (When we say 'look *back*, we mean that literally; start with where you are now, and work backwards.)

Obviously, it's for you to decide what makes a key event. It may be something that sticks in your memory—or conversely you may have tried to forget it, so you might need to think a bit. (But don't worry about trying to remember everything. You can always come back and add some more later, when recollections occur to you, as they are almost bound to when you get into some of the later steps.)

Perhaps most events will be things that happened quickly, in a definitely identifiable short space of time. Others, however, may have carried on much longer—for weeks or even months. The important thing is that you can recognize the experience as a specific happening in your life.

We can't possibly say how many such events you should try to identify; it depends on so many factors. So if there's not enough space here, use a separate sheet of paper.

Step 2. Life-line

Now take a sheet of paper and draw a 'graph' of your life so far, with time along the bottom axis, and feelings up the side. So, when you were feeling good, you would have a peak; and when you were feeling bad, there would be a trough (see Fig. 3.1).

This 'graph' can be as detailed as you like, covering your whole life to date or a particular period.

SHARING: If you are working with a partner, now is the time to share your events and life-line. Talk about them with each other. What happened? How did you feel? What did you want to do? What did you do?

Step 3. Periods

Now look over your list of events, and your life-line. Working forwards this time (i.e., starting from way back, coming towards the present), look at the periods between events, and give them a label or title that describes how they were, what they felt like, what their purpose was, and so on. Mark these titles of periods in on your life-line.

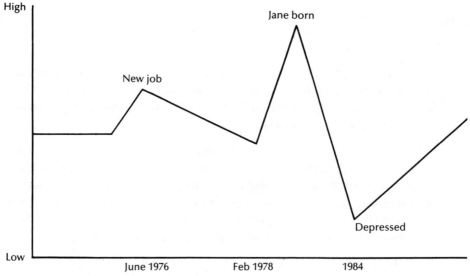

Figure 3.1. Life-line graph

Step 4. Collage

Next, get hold of a collection of old magazines, newspapers, travel brochures and so on. Using these, and bearing in mind your list of events and your life-line, cut out pictures, words, letters (or parts of these) that represent the way you think and feel about your life so far. Take a large sheet of paper and stick these cut out bits on it with glue, thus forming a collage or picture of your whole life.

SHARING: Now is the time to share with your partner again. Talk about each other's collage. What does yours mean to you?

Step 5. Themes

Now look over the picture that is emerging of your life so far—that is, at your list of events and periods, at your life-line, and at your collage. From all of these, what *themes* can you see emerging? Perhaps it would be useful if we say a bit more about what we mean by 'theme' in this context. For example, it might be:

- a pattern of thoughts, feelings, happenings, behaviours that crop up at regular intervals, or in certain circumstances, or after certain other happenings, etc.;
- an aspect (or aspects) of your life or of yourself that seems to be there all the time;
- an aspect (or aspects) of your life or of yourself that makes itself apparent from time to time (perhaps in one of the patterns mentioned earlier).

The main point here is to *identify* your themes; in the next step you will be able to think about what these may mean to you, what they are saying to you.

SHARING: This is now a useful time for further sharing with a partner. Indeed, by this stage you may well be in a position to give feedback to each other about themes you think you may have spotted in each other's biographies.

Step 6. Achievements

At this point it is useful to see what you have achieved so far; list up to ten things that you think you have achieved, or that describe you or your life to far, with regard to:

(a) Your FAMILY, FRIENDS, and OTHER PERSONAL RELATION-SHIPS

(b) Your CAREER

(c) Your MATERIAL WEALTH and POSSESSIONS

(d) Your HEALTH, PERSONAL DEVELOPMENT, and LEARNING

(e) Your SPIRITUAL DEVELOPMENT

What do you think of these lists? How do they make you feel? (If you are working with a partner, *share* your lists and your feelings.)

The present

Step 7. Questions and issues coming your way

So far, then, you have looked at events, periods, themes, and achievements from the past, together with getting an overall picture of your life so far. You can now move into the present by looking at questions and issues coming your way.

We suggest three ways of identifying these. As before, you will find the process works better if you *share* with a partner as you go along.

1. *The overall picture of your life so far.* If your biography were someone else's, and he or she was describing it to you, how would you react to it? What would you think about it? How would you feel? What do you see as that person's unfinished business, or next tasks? What decisions need to be faced? What is coming his or her way?

   Then, of course, remember that it is in fact your biography. These are *your* issues. Write them down.

2. *Themes.* Look at your themes—these can very often give a good indication of some of the questions and issues coming your way. For example, there may be themes that:

have always been there	]
or	] What do these patterns
appear from time to time	] mean to you? How do you
or	] feel about them?
are only now emerging	]

	[weaker, lessened?
	[or
Would you like the feeling	[removed, finished with?
to be	[or
	[stronger, decreased?

3. *People in your consciousness.* We all carry around in our consciousness a 'network' of people. Many of these will be people we interact with in our lives at present—members of our family, friends, colleagues, rivals, etc. Others may be people we haven't seen for a long time, but whom nevertheless we remember and think about, and who thus still influence us. Some of these may no longer be alive—or perhaps were never even born (e.g. the

daughter I never had). As long as they are in our 'consciousness net', they are probably saying things to us, or asking us questions. So, draw up a list of people in your consciousness (actually some may be more or less subconscious memories; think back into your biography), and identify what it is they are saying to you, or asking you.

The future

Step 8. Unachieved goals

You have drawn up a list of achievements—what about things that you have not yet achieved? (Again, of course, *sharing* is recommended.)

(a) Write your own obituary as you would like it to appear in a newspaper or journal of your choice.

(b) Think of a perfect day some time in the future; it includes all those things in it that you would like for yourself. Imagine it in some detail. Who else is there? What are you doing? How does it feel? What are the others doing? What are their feelings?

(c) What as yet unrealized goals do you have in respect of:

● Your FAMILY, FRIENDS, and OTHER PERSONAL RELATION-
   SHIPS?

● Your CAREER?

● Your MATERIAL WEALTH and POSSESSIONS?

● Your HEALTH, PERSONAL DEVELOPMENT, and LEARNING?

●Your SPIRITUAL DEVELOPMENT?

●OTHER GOALS

Step 9. Intentions

By now, then, you have a considerable amount of data about yourself, your biography, issues and questions coming your way, and unachieved goals. From these you need to select something to work on, to choose as a priority.

Obviously, only you can decide where your priorities lie. As a first attempt, look over your data and select say five or six areas, questions or issues to start with.

A good way of proceeding from this point is to use a technique known as *domain mapping*. This starts with a diagram like that shown in Fig. 3.2 which is basically made up of a series of rings, like a dart board, with you at the centre. You then divide the 'board' up into a number of sections (segments, to be precise) or 'domains', one for each area/question/issue that you have chosen to explore further. You identify each of these domains by writing a short 'label' in the second ring. (Our example just shows a couple of domains.)

In the next ring you write a brief description of the way you are with that particular aspect of your life—be it a relationship with a person, or with a task, or with part of yourself, or whatever. In this way you end up with a concise overview of the current position with the five or six issues that you have chosen to focus on.

Now for your *intentions*. Decide which you are going to work on (probably no more than two or three in the first instance) and in the next ring write in how you would like things to be as far as that domain is concerned.

Step 10. Alternative courses of action

Having identified and written down your desired intentions, how are you going to set about achieving these?

For most issues there will always be several possible ways, each with its pros and cons. This is another case of when it will clearly depend

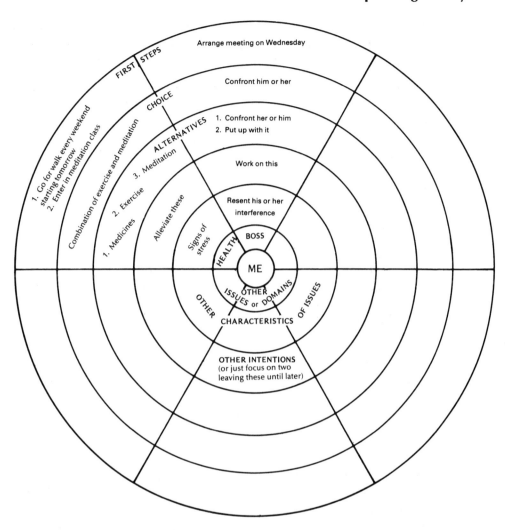

Figure 3.2. Domain mapping

on you and the nature of your questions, although you might find it useful to bear in mind that there are four general alternatives when faced with an intolerable situation, namely:

change the situation: do something about it, be proactive;
change yourself: examine your own attitudes, behaviour, skills, etc., and change them as appropriate;
change your relationship with the situation: that is, come to terms with it, decide to live with it, grin and bear it;
leave the situation: find a constructive way of moving on.

Here again, working with a partner can be extremely useful, as you can share and help each other to generate alternatives. You can also think together over the relative advantages and disadvantages of each alternative, thus enabling you to *choose* one particular course of action. This choice is then written in the next ring of the diagram.

(Incidentally, a useful technique to help with this choice is called *force field analysis*, and is described in Part 2, Activity No. 15. And you can use a variation of something you have already done, namely, imagining a day in the future (Step 8b), although in this case you imagine, in turn, that you have taken each of the alternatives. What's happening? Who else is there? What are you doing? What are they doing? How are you and they feeling?)

Step 11. Planning first steps

Finally, you are now approaching the actual implementation of your chosen course of action. So think about your first steps—when are you going to start? What opportunities for the action will present themselves? What opportunities or conditions will you need to create? What will you actually do? How? Write this in the final ring of the domain map.

Keeping going. 'The best laid plans . . .' So you'll need to review your progress from time to time, updating your domain map, coming back to it, identifying new issues and so on. Living—and life planning—is a continuous process.

FURTHER READING

Many of the books which look at the biographical issues which face us all at one time or another focus upon work or career. Richard Bolles' *What Colour is your Parachute?* (Umbrella Publishing Services, 1985) is a classic for job-seekers. Dave Francis' *Managing Your Own Career* (Fontana, 1985) is a useful little book with lots of self-assessment activities. More broadly, another classic, Gail Sheehy's *Passages: Predictable Crises of Adult Life* (Corgi, 1977) is as fresh as paint. Bernard Lievegoed's *Phases: Crisis and Development in the Individual* (Rudolf Steiner Press, 2nd edn, 1982) is our own touchstone.

4 Some ideas about management and the qualities of successful managers

This book is a programme of activities for self-development based on our ideas of what contributes to successful managing. Before going on to outline these ideas, you might like to pause here and jot down your own views so that you can compare them with ours.

What do you think:

- are the main features of a manager's job, and what *is* management?
- are the main qualities required to be a successful manager?

We use a framework of what we call the qualities of the effective manager. This framework comes from a research project carried out by one of us and from our own experience and wide reading about management and the nature of managerial work.

The research project identified a number of qualities which were found more often in successful managers than in those who were judged to be less successful. Successful managers were those who had risen to senior posts, or who were significantly younger on average for their level of seniority ('whizz-kids'), or, most importantly, managers of any age or level who were seen as doing their jobs with above average effectiveness.[1]

The research identified 10 attributes which were found to be possessed by the successful managers, and since then we have added another. These 11 qualities, or attributes, form the basis of the programme of self-development provided in this book:

1. Command of basic facts
2. Relevant professional knowledge
3. Continuing sensitivity to events
4. Analytical, problem-solving, decision/judgement-making skills
5. Social skills and abilities
6. Emotional resilience
7. Proactivity—inclination to respond purposefully to events

23

8. Creativity
9. Mental agility
10. Balanced learning habits and skills
11. Self-knowledge

These qualities fall into three groups, which constitute three different levels. Numbers 1 and 2 form the foundation level: they represent two kinds of basic knowledge and information that a manager may need to use in making decisions and taking action.

Numbers 3 to 7 are specific skills and attributes that directly affect behaviour and performance. Number 3 is the skill or quality that allows managers to acquire the basic knowledge and information involved in 1 and 2.

Numbers 8 to 11 are those qualities which allow the manager to develop and deploy skills and resources in categories 3, 4, and 5. They may be called 'meta-qualities' because they allow the manager to develop the situation-specific skills needed in particular circumstances. (See Fig. 4.1.)

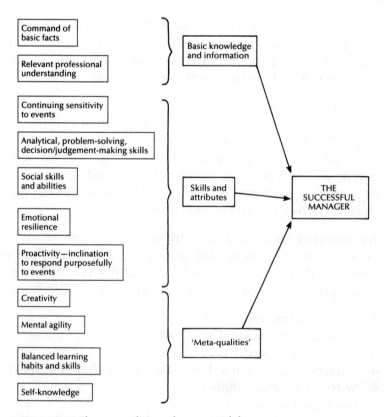

Figure 4.1. Eleven qualities of a successful manager

Many of the attributes are interconnected—that is, possession of one contributes to possession of another.

Below is a short explanation of each of these 11 attributes, providing our basic model for self-development.

Basic knowledge and information

1. Command of basic facts

Successful managers know what's what in their organization. They have a command of such basic facts as goals and plans (long- and short-term), product knowledge, who's who in the organization, the roles and relationships between various departments, their own job and what's expected of them. If they don't store all this information, they know where to get it when they need it.

2. Relevant professional knowledge

This category includes 'technical' knowledge, e.g., production technology, marketing techniques, engineering knowledge, relevant legislation, sources of finance, and knowledge of basic background management principles and theories, e.g., planning, organizing, and controlling.

Skills

3. Continuing sensitivity to events

Managers vary in the degree to which they can sense what is happening in a particular situation. The successful manager is relatively sensitive to events and can tune in to what's going on and is perceptive and open to information—'hard' information, such as facts and figures, and 'soft' information, such as the feelings of other people. The manager with this sensitivity is able to respond in an appropriate way to situations as they arise.

4. Analytical, problem-solving, and decision/judgement-making skills

The job of the manager is very much concerned with making decisions. Sometimes these can be made using logical, optimizing techniques. Other decisions call for the ability to weight pros and cons in what is basically a very uncertain or ambiguous situation, calling for a high level of judgement or even intuition. The manager must therefore develop judgement-making skills, including the ability to cope with ambiguity and uncertainty, striking a balance between the necessity at times to be guided by subjective feelings without throwing objective logic completely out of the window.

5. *Social skills and abilities*

One definition of management often cited is 'getting things done through other people'. This definition may be inadequate, but it does point to one of the key features of the manager's job—it requires interpersonal skills. The successful manager develops a range of abilities which are essential in such activities: communicating, delegating, negotiating, resolving conflict, persuading, selling, using and responding to authority and power.

Personal qualities

6. *Emotional resilience*

The manager's job involves a degree of emotional stress and strain, which arises as a natural consequence of working in situations involving authority, leadership, power, interpersonal conflict, meeting targets and deadlines, all within a framework of a degree of uncertainty and ambiguity.

The successful manager needs to be sufficiently resilient to cope with this. 'Resilient' means that, when feeling stressed we don't get thick-skinned and insensitive, but manage to cope by maintaining self-control and by 'giving' to some extent.

7. *Proactivity—inclination to respond purposefully to events*

Effective managers have some purpose or goal to achieve, rather than merely responding to demand. They cannot plan everything carefully in advance, and at times they must respond to the needs of the instant situation, but when making such a response the effective manager is able to consider the longer term. Immediate responses are related to overall and longer-term aims and goals, whereas the less successful manager responds in a relatively unthinking or uncritical way to the immediate pressure. This category of ability also includes such qualities as seeing a job through, being dedicated and committed, having a sense of mission, and taking responsibility for things that happen rather than passing the buck to someone else.

8. *Creativity*

By 'creativity' we mean the ability to come up with unique new responses to situations, and to have the breadth of insight to recognize and take up useful new approaches. It involves not only having new ideas oneself, but also the ability to recognize a good idea when it is presented from another source.

9. *Mental agility*

Although related to general intelligence level, the concept of 'mental agility' includes the ability to grasp problems quickly, to think of several things at once, to switch rapidly from one problem or situation to another, to see quickly the whole situation (rather than ponderously plough through all its components), and to 'think on one's feet'. Given the hectic nature of managerial work these are particularly necessary qualities for success.

10. *Balanced learning habits and skills*

Data collected by observing and interviewing managers show that a significant proportion of the degree of their success can be explained by the presence or absence of habits and skills related to learning.

- Successful managers are more independent as learners; they take responsibility for the 'rightness' of what is learned, rather than depending, passively and uncritically, on an authority figure (a teacher or an expert) to define 'truths'.
- Successful managers are capable of abstract thinking, as well as concrete, practical thought. They are able to relate concrete ideas to abstract ones (and vice versa) relatively quickly. This ability—which is sometimes known as a 'helicopter mind'—enables managers to generate their own theories from practice, and to develop their own practical ideas from theory.
- The ability to use a range of different learning processes is necessary for managerial success. Three such processes are:
  (a) input—receiving expository teaching, either formal (e.g., on a course) or informal (e.g., coaching by a colleague);
  (b) discovery—generating personal meaning from one's own experiences;
  (c) reflection—a process of analysing and reorganizing pre-existing experiences and ideas.
- Successful managers are more likely to have a relatively wide view of the nature of the skills of management. For example, they are more likely to recognize the range of managerial attributes as presented in this model, than to believe that management is a unitary activity, involving, for example, dealing with staff members (i.e., needing only a certain set of social skills) or simply involving basic decision making.

11. *Self-knowledge*

Whatever each of us does is affected by our own view of our job or role, by our goals, values, feelings, strengths, weaknesses, and a host of other personal factors. To keep a relatively high degree of self-control, the manager must be aware of these self-attributes and the part they play in influencing actions. The successful manager therefore needs skills of introspection.

Qualities or competencies?

Over the last few years in the world of management training and development, considerable efforts have been made to identify 'competencies' for a range of jobs, including that of the manager. A

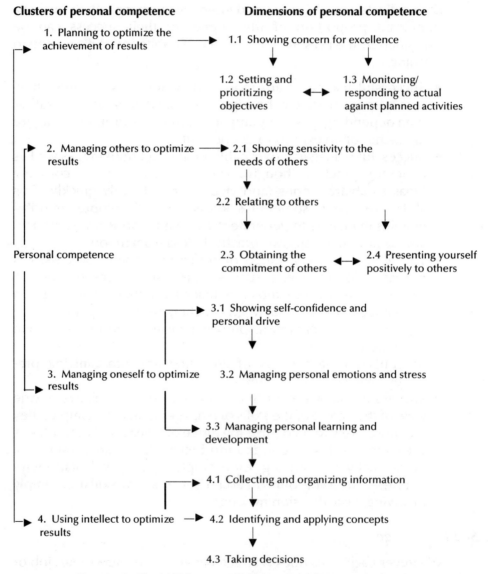

Figure 4.2. The MCI framework of managerial competencies

model of managerial competencies published by the Management Charter Initiative (MCI) is reproduced in Fig. 4.2. It is interesting to see close parallels with our own, earlier model as used in this book (Fig. 4.3).

MCI competencies	*Eleven qualities of the effective manager*
1.1 Showing concern for excellence	7 Proactivity—inclination to respond purposefully to events and 2 Relevant professional knowledge
1.2 Setting and prioritizing objectives	4 Analytical, problem-solving, decision/judgement-making skills
1.3 Monitoring/responding to actual against planned activities	3 Continuing sensitivity to events
2.1 Showing sensitivity to the needs of others	3 Continuing sensitivity to events and 5 Social skills and abilities
2.2 Relating to others	5 Social skills and abilities
2.3 Obtaining the commitment of others	5 Social skills and abilities
2.4 Presenting yourself positively to others	5 Social skills and abilities and 7 Proactivity—inclination to respond purposefully to events
3.1 Showing self-confidence and personal drive	7 Proactivity—inclination to respond purposefully to events
3.2 Managing personal emotions and stress	6 Emotional resilience
3.3 Managing personal learning and development	10 Balanced learning habits
4.1 Collecting and organizing information	1 Command of basic facts and 4 Analytical, problem-solving, decision/judgement-making skills
4.2 Identifying and applying concepts	9 Mental agility and 10 Balanced learning habits
4.3 Taking decisions	4 Analytical, problem-solving, decision/judgement-making skills
No MCI equivalents →	8 Creativity
→	11 Self-knowledge

Figure 4.3. MCI competencies and the eleven qualities of the effective manager

Our view of qualities of competencies is that it is useful to have frameworks to give people an idea of the kinds of knowledge, skills, abilities and so on that may be appropriate in a given job, but that it is misleading to use any such framework rigidly. The person doing this job should be the final judge of what is useful to him or her in performing effectively. We offer the eleven qualities of effective managers as a guide—take it or leave it, take some of it, modify it, add to it, it's up to you.

No-one is against competence, a wholly admirable thing to give or to receive. The dangers appear, especially in the sort of discretionary work which most of us do these days, when *single, external measures* are used to define competence and, by implication, incompetence. All skills and abilities are *personal qualities*, learned, exercised and owned by individual people. The provider and the receiver of a service may define competence, incompetence or excellence in a way which does not make sense outside that context.

Finally, while we're interested in helping people become more competent, we're also interested in performance which goes beyond one meaning of this word. For people whose standards of work are well beyond the norm, the word 'competent' is an insult. Such people—and they are found in every field of life and work—deserve the accolade of artist, their work being a personal expression of their inner and outer qualities.

Summary: So what?

One of the fundamental beliefs underlying this book is that everything written here is our opinion. It is essential, if the book is to succeed as an aid to your self-development, that you decide the extent to which you share our opinions, and what they mean, personally, to you.

Therefore, having read this chapter, write down your reactions to it. How do you feel already about what we have written? Interested? Bored? Sceptical? Enthusiastic? In agreement? In disagreement? Do our views match yours? What are your other reactions?

One of the activities (Activity 6) involves the keeping of a personal journal, the idea being to keep note of your on-going experiences, to identify your feelings about these experiences, and so learn from them. You may consider that reading these first chapters is an experience right for inclusion in the journal; if so, we suggest you work through Activity 6 now, before proceeding further.

REFERENCES

1. Burgoyne, J. G. and R. Stuart, 'The nature, use and acquisition of managerial skills and other attributes', *Personnel Review*, 5(4), 1976, pp. 19–29.

5 Assessing yourself and setting some goals for self-development

In Chapter 4 we described our model of the qualities of effective managers. As we explained, we are using this model as the basis around which to build the activities which form the second part of this book.

One way of approaching the activities is to work through them in the order in which they appear. A better alternative is to determine your own priority areas and concentrate first on these. This chapter describes ways in which you might do this, involving three stages:

- diagnosis
- goal setting
- planning for on-going evaluation

Different people will prefer different methods—it is up to each person to choose a preference. You might like to try out more than one method; if so, it will be interesting to compare the results to see to what extent they differ or concur.

Method One: simple introspection

Step 1. Diagnosis

The 11 qualities of effective managers are listed in column 1 of Table 5.1. Consider yourself in terms of each quality in turn. How well equipped are you in each case? How much of the quality do you possess and to what extent would you like to develop it further? Think carefully about this. To help with this process, Table 5.1 presents you with some questions which you can ask yourself in connection with each of the 11 areas.

Step 2. Goal setting

Look over your answers. Do any areas stand out in which you feel you are particularly lacking in skills or abilities? Or are your scores more or less the same for each of the 11 qualities?

Quality	Indicative questions
1. Command of basic facts	—How much do you know about what's going on in your organization? —What are you sources of information? —How extensive are your contacts? —How many people do you know in your organization? —What do you know about the way other people feel about your organization? 'Other people' should include those superior to you, at your own level, more junior to yourself, owners, management, and workforce; customers, consumers, and clients. —Can you think of some recent examples of occasions when you needed to know more basic facts? —How much do you know about your organization's policies? —How much do you know about your organization's medium- and long-term plans? —What do you do to keep informed about all these things?
2. Relevant professional knowledge	—What do you do to keep up to date with new techniques and with the latest thinking in your area? —How much time do you spend reading specialist journals? —How do you get guidance on technical or specialist aspects of your job? —How well-informed are you about possible legislative, governmental, and international changes, and the effect these might have on your organization?
3. Continuing sensitivity to events	—What do you do to make sure that you are tuned in to what's happening in a given situation? —How sensitive are you to the way other people are feeling, or to the way in which they are likely to react? What steps do you take to develop this sensitivity? —How perceptive are you? —How do you make sure that your assumptions about what's going on are correct? —What types of situation do you find hardest to weigh up?

Table 5.1. Some indicative questions to help you to give yourself a self-rating on the 11 qualities of an effective manager

Quality	Indicative questions
4. Problem-solving, analytical, and decision/judgement-making skills	—What do you find most difficult about making decisions? —How do you feel about having to make judgements in situations in which ideally you would have more information? —What range of decision-making techniques do you have available to help you when appropriate? —Can you think of some recent examples of good and bad decisions you made? —In general, how confident are you in your decision-making abilities?
5. Social skills and abilities	—How much difficulty do you have with other people? What types of such difficulty do you have? —What do you do in situations involving inter-personal conflict? —Can you think of some recent examples of situations in which you needed to use social skills? What happened? —How much do you know about what other people think and feel about you? —How do you respond to anger, hostility, suspicion? —How do you try to ensure that other people understand you when you communicate with them? How do you ensure that you understand others?
6. Emotional resilience	—How do you cope with feelings of stress, tension, anxiety, fatigue? —With whom do you discuss your worries and anxieties? —Think of the most tense, stressful situations that you have been in recently. How did you behave? —What do you do when you become emotional? —How do you behave in situations of great ambiguity? (i.e., when you don't know what's going to happen next, when everything seems very uncertain). Can you give some examples? —What do you do to make sure that you neither become thick-skinned nor over-affected by emotions?

Table 5.1. continued

Quality	Indicative questions
7. Proactivity—inclination to respond purpose-fully to events	—What steps do you take to ensure that you're in control of your own behaviour, rather than allowing yourself to be controlled or manipulated by others or by situational pressures? —In which situations do you tend to be independent and proactive as compared with situations in which you tend to be dependent and reactive? —How good are you at taking the initiative? —To what extent are you thrusting, active, self-starting, rather than sleeping, passive, following?
8. Creativity	—How easy do you find it to come up with new ideas? —How do you feel when all the well-tried solutions to a problem have failed? —What do you do to try to see new ways of doing things? —How often do you try out new methods, approaches, and solutions to problems? —What are the most creative things you have done in the past 12 months? —How often do you get seemingly crazy ideas which, on further development, turn out to be good and useful?
9. Mental agility	—How good are you at coping with several problems or tasks at the same time? —Can you think of a few examples of situations in which you really needed to think quickly? What happened in each case? —How often do you get sudden flashes of insight, in which 'all the pieces seem to come together' to solve a problem? Can you think of some examples of this? —How do you feel when faced with the need for rapid thinking? —What do you do when faced with seemingly contradictory information, data, or ideas?

Table 5.1. continued

Quality	Indicative questions

10. Balanced learning habits and skills	—How good are you at relating theory and practice in management?
	—Can you think of examples of occasions when you were able to draw general conclusions, or generate mini-theories, from your own practical experiences?
	—Can you think of examples of occasions on which you
	  (a) preferred to rely on the guidance of an expert rather than trust your own judgement? and
	  (b) preferred to trust you own judgement rather than rely on the guidance of an expert?
	—What do you do to ensure that you use a balanced range of learning habits?

11. Self-knowledge	—What do you do to increase your level of self-knowledge? —Can you give examples of instances when knowledge or understanding of how you were feeling or behaving affected what you were doing? —To what extent are you consciously aware of your own goals, values, beliefs, feelings, behaviour? —How often do you stop to consider your own behaviour, its causes and effects?

Table 5.1. continued

If one or two stand out clearly, choose these as your first priorities. If they are all more or less the same, select a couple either at random, or which particularly appeal to you.

However you choose them, concentrate on one or two areas only. You can come back to the others later.

When you have chosen your one or two priority areas, give yourself a specific goal; for example:

'By   (choose a realistic date by which you hope to have achieved this goal) I will have carried out all (or 50 per cent or whatever) of the activities, provided that they are related to this goal area.'*

*Chapter 6 provides a means of identifying which activities are related to which goal areas.

Step 3. Planning for on-going evaluation

It is important to recognize that self-development must be a continuous process. For this reason, the activities presented in Part 2 of this book are designed so that most of them can become incorporated into your everyday way of doing things.

Review your progress and set new goals as time proceeds. When your target date arrives, evaluate your progress against your goals and decide what further action to take, if any. This then becomes a cycle (Fig. 5.1).

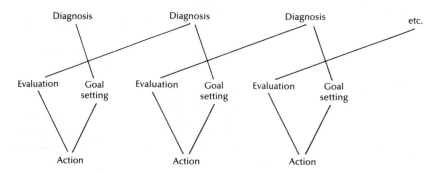

Figure 5.1

You can then continue with new goals and, in due course, further self-ratings, goals, self-ratings, goals, etc., *ad infinitum*. We use this phrase advisedly, since the ideal is that you incorporate this way of thinking, diagnosing, and goal setting into your everyday activities as a manager, hence increasing your effectiveness. It is, of course, important to be honest with yourself when diagnosing your needs; since there are no points to be scored or exams to be passed, the only person you will be cheating if you are not honest will be yourself.

Method Two: conversation with a partner

Although this book is designed so that you can work through it on your own, it will be helpful to work with somebody else. An appropriate partner may give useful feedback, challenge assumptions, provide support, help sound out ideas.

The partner must be committed to the role. An ideal situation would be one in which you and a colleague both undertake a programme of self-development, so that you can each act as helper to the other.

For those who are able to work with a partner, we present this second method for self-diagnosis and goal setting. In essence it is the same as Method One, with the additional factor that you discuss each step with your partner.

Step 1. Diagnosis

Using the indicative questions given in Table 5.1, take each quality of the effective manager in turn and discuss it with your partner. How well equipped are you? To what extent do you want to develop this quality further? Think about these questions and get your partner's views and compare them with your own.

Step 2. Goal setting

This is as Step 2 in Method One—but again, work with your partner by sharing your conclusions and goals.

Step 3. Planning for on-going evaluation

Again, this is as in Method One (Step 3), but is done collaboratively, with your partner.

Method Three: self-administered questionnaire

The first two methods have been relatively open-ended. They required you to think, in only a semistructured way, about yourself in relation to the qualities of an effective manager, and then rate yourself on a four-point scale.

The third method is more structured in that it uses a specific set of questions, with a predetermined scoring scheme.

Step 1. Diagnosis

The questionnaire below contains 110 questions. Table 5.2 is designed as a means of scoring your answers to the questionnaire.

For each of the 110 statements, you tick or circle, in the respective cell or box of Table 5.2, (a), (b), (c), or (d). The answer scheme is:

(a) Mark (a) if you think that the statement is *definitely not true* of you; you *strongly disagree* with the statement; you *never behave or feel* the way indicated by the statement.
(b) Mark (b) if you think that the statement is *sometimes true* of you; you *partly agree* with the statement; you *sometimes behave or feel* the way indicated by the statement.

(c) Mark (c) if you think that the statement is *generally true* of you; you *definitely agree* with the statement; you *quite often behave or feel* the way indicated by the statement.

(d) Mark (d) if you think that the statement is *always, or very nearly always,* true of you; you *strongly agree* with the statement; you *usually or always behave or feel* the way indicated by the statement.

Instructions for calculating your results are given after Table 5.2.

THE QUESTIONNAIRE

1. I find I don't know enough about what's going on around me.
2. I find that I don't know enough about the technical aspects of my job.
3. I don't seem able to pick up quickly what's going on.
4. I dither when faced with a decision.
5. I find that other people don't listen to me properly.
6. I try to be objective and not to worry about my feelings.
7. I respond to the pressures of the instant, thus losing sight of longer-term considerations.
8. I find it difficult to come up with new ideas.
9. Compared with other people, I'm rather slow on the uptake.
10. I don't see much connection between theory and practice in management.
11. I find it difficult to ask other people what they really think of me.
12. I make plans or decisions only to find later on that they are no longer valid because of something that I should have known but didn't.
13. Many of the people working with or for me seem to know more about various aspects of the job than I do.
14. I'm not very good at knowing or recognizing what other people are thinking or feeling.
15. I have difficulty in analysing a situation into its various aspects.
16. There are times when I just don't seem to be able to get other people to see my point of view.
17. I get worried because there's no way of knowing in advance whether or not I have made the right decision.
18. I find that after a while there's no point in keeping up a losing struggle.
19. I'm not an imaginative person.
20. I have difficulty in thinking on my feet in tricky situations.
21. Experience is the only valid teacher.
22. It's dangerous to be introspective.

23. I get caught out because I don't know what's happening in my organization.
24. I would like to be more up to date on the technical aspects of my job.
25. I find that when something happens I'm only aware of part of what's going on—I overlook other aspects of the situation or problem.
26. I find it difficulty to weigh up the pros and cons of a solution to a problem.
27. Anger and conflict tend to frighten or upset me.
28. I have difficulty in sleeping at night.
29. It's difficult to think very far ahead, since the immediate goal is more important.
30. I don't think that people with other specialist interests have much to offer me in my particular job.
31. I prefer to work on one thing at a time rather than be dealing with several things at once.
32. I'm not able to convert my own experiences into valid theories.
33. There's just not enough time in my job to sit around talking about how we feel about each other.
34. People don't seem to tell me enough about what's going on in the organization.
35. It would help me in my job if I could learn more about relevant techniques.
36. Other people seem to notice more than I do about what's happening around them.
37. I tend to jump to instant conclusions—acting quickly without spending much time thinking.
38. I avoid telling people what I really think about them.
39. When I'm nervous or tired I snap at people or get moody and irritable.
40. I'm passive rather than active.
41. My job is unique, so I don't think that people from other backgrounds could be of much help to me.
42. Once I get stuck into a task I try to remain with it rather than switch to something else and then back again.
43. I don't sit and think abstract thoughts about management.
44. I'm basically a logical person, and I don't let my feelings influence me.
45. I find that I need more information about the organization but don't know how to get it.
46. I am not very well versed in the range of techniques that could be relevant to my job.
47. I don't really feel tuned-in to what's happening in a situation.

48. I find it difficult to trust my own judgement.
49. I find myself irritated by other people.
50. I don't think that feelings should be brought into issues.
51. I need to temper initiative with caution.
52. I am better at implementing well-tried solutions rather than experimenting with new ones.
53. To see the whole situation one must carefully consider all the parts.
54. It's best to rely on experts when seeking ideas about specialized aspects of one's job.
55. I don't think we should let our values and feelings affect the way we behave at work.
56. I don't have a clear understanding of how my organization works.
57. I would like to have more theoretical knowledge that would help me in my job.
58. I have difficulty in knowing what other people are up to.
59. Having made up my mind about something I like to get somebody else's opinion about my decision.
60. I don't really know what others think of me.
61. I don't get emotional in my job—I just stick to the facts.
62. I find it difficult to stick at it when things aren't going too well.
63. I get mental blockages when trying to think of new ways of doing things.
64. 'Slow and steady wins the race' is a pretty good motto.
65. When I get an idea I like, if possible, to have it checked out by an expert.
66. My medium- and long-term ambitions are not clear.
67. I have difficulty in getting all the information I need.
68. I find that I don't seem to know enough about external factors such as market changes, new legislation, and the like.
69. I find myself surprised because I've only been seeing 'part of the picture'.
70. I would like some sort of a formula that I could apply to problems so as to work out the best solution or decision.
71. I usually lose arguments.
72. I find myself aware that I'm behaving inappropriately, but don't seem to be able to stop or change the way I'm acting.
73. I feel a need to have more 'get-up-and-go'.
74. I have difficulty in coming up with new ideas.
75. I can't cope with more than one or two problems at a time.
76. If I go on a course I would like the teachers or trainers to be able to give me a lot of information and ideas.
77. There's not much point in thinking about oneself and 'contemplating one's navel'.

78. Many of my colleagues seem to know more about the organization than I do.
79. I have difficulty in keeping up with new techniques and developments.
80. If people change their hair-styles, or the way they dress, I probably wouldn't notice.
81. I get confused when faced with several alternative courses of action.
82. I don't really see it as part of my job to step in between two people who don't get on with each other, as long as they do their job satisfactorily.
83. I worry about problems over and over in my mind.
84. If forced to choose between two descriptions of myself, I would say that I am steady and reliable rather than adventurous and risk-taking.
85. Other people seem better than me at thinking of new ways of solving problems.
86. I'm not what you'd call a quick thinker.
87. If I hear of a new theory I find it difficult to translate it into practical terms relevant to my job.
88. I wouldn't like other people to tell me exactly what they think of me.
89. I don't really know who the important people are in my organization.
90. I would welcome the opportunity to learn more about the theoretical background to by job.
91. I have difficulty in knowing how other people are feeling.
92. When trying to make a decision I find that I've got so much information that I don't know what to do with it.
93. I find that I simply cannot understand why someone else feels the way he does.
94. I don't discuss my feelings or worries with other people.
95. I prefer to follow someone else's plans or instructions rather than act on my own initiative.
96. I don't seem as good as other people at getting creative ideas.
97. The trouble with my job is that I'm never left alone to get on with it—there are too many interruptions.
98. I dislike jargon or over-theoretical ways of talking.
99. It's a good job we can't read the thoughts of others.
100. I would like to know more about my organization's policies and future plans.
101. I am not really sufficiently *au fait* with the technical requirements of my job.
102. I find myself surprised at the way other people react to what's happening.

103. I tend to find that I can't make a decision because I don't have enough relevant information.
104. Many of the people in my organization can't be trusted to get on with their job without constant supervision.
105. Most days I wake up with a 'Monday-morning' feeling.
106. It's better to be safe than sorry.
107. Compared with other people, my ideas seem to be stuck in a rut, or fixed by well-established ways of doing things.
108. When I'm under pressure, in a tight spot, or being challenged, I can't seem to think straight or express my ideas clearly.
109. I'm the sort of person who goes around saying 'no one can tell me how to do my job'.
110. I don't spend much time thinking about myself—my strengths and weaknesses.

SCORING THE QUESTIONNAIRE

To calculate your score, take the first *column* of Table 5.2 (i.e., squares corresponding to questions 1, 12, 23, 34, 45, 56, 67, 78, 89, and 100) and give yourself points as follows:

2 points for every (a) marked*
1 point for every (b) marked
2 points for every (c) marked
3 points for every (d) marked

Then add up the total number of points scored in column 1, and write this in the space marked 'A' at the foot of the column.

This procedure should then be repeated for each of the other columns, with totals written in spaces B to K.

The 11 columns (and spaces A to K) correspond to the 11 qualities of an effective manager. The questionnaire is written in such a way that the higher your score, the more you seem to have a self-development need in respect of that quality.

Step 2. Goal setting

First, transfer your scores from Table 5.2 to column 1 of Table 5.3. When you have done this, look over your scores. Are there any that stand out as being higher than others, or are they all more or less the same?

*Although, in theory, an 'a' should incur no points—as it implies no fault or even perfection—it does in fact score 2, the reason being that if you really do come up to 'a' standard you don't need this book; if you don't then you're blind to your faults by putting 'a's down.

1 a b c d	2 a b c d	3 a b c d	4 a b c d	5 a b c d	6 a b c d	7 a b c d	8 a b c d	9 a b c d	10 a b c d	11 a b c d
12 a b c d	13 a b c d	14 a b c d	15 a b c d	16 a b c d	17 a b c d	18 a b c d	19 a b c d	20 a b c d	21 a b c d	22 a b c d
23 a b c d	24 a b c d	25 a b c d	26 a b c d	27 a b c d	28 a b c d	29 a b c d	30 a b c d	31 a b c d	32 a b c d	33 a b c d
34 a b c d	35 a b c d	36 a b c d	37 a b c d	38 a b c d	39 a b c d	40 a b c d	41 a b c d	42 a b c d	43 a b c d	44 a b c d
45 a b c d	46 a b c d	47 a b c d	48 a b c d	49 a b c d	50 a b c d	51 a b c d	52 a b c d	53 a b c d	54 a b c d	55 a b c d
56 a b c d	57 a b c d	58 a b c d	59 a b c d	60 a b c d	61 a b c d	62 a b c d	63 a b c d	64 a b c d	65 a b c d	66 a b c d
67 a b c d	68 a b c d	69 a b c d	70 a b c d	71 a b c d	72 a b c d	73 a b c d	74 a b c d	75 a b c d	76 a b c d	77 a b c d
78 a b c d	79 a b c d	80 a b c d	81 a b c d	82 a b c d	83 a b c d	84 a b c d	85 a b c d	86 a b c d	87 a b c d	88 a b c d
89 a b c d	90 a b c d	91 a b c d	92 a b c d	93 a b c d	94 a b c d	95 a b c d	96 a b c d	97 a b c d	98 a b c d	99 a b c d
100 a b c d	101 a b c d	102 a b c d	103 a b c d	104 a b c d	105 a b c d	106 a b c d	107 a b c d	108 a b c d	109 a b c d	110 a b c d
A	B	C	D	E	F	G	H	I	J	K

Table 5.2. For use with self-diagnosis Method Three: self-administered questionnaire

If one or two are definitely higher than others, then it would probably be a good idea to choose these as your priorities to start on. If they are all about the same, however, then you might as well choose one or two either at random or by selecting areas that particularly appeal to you.

In any case, we suggest that at this stage you concentrate on one or two areas only; you can come back to the others later.

When you have chosen your one or two priority areas, try to give yourself a reasonably specific goal, for example:

'By   (choose a realistic date by which you hope to have achieved this goal) I will have carried out all (or 50 per cent, or whatever) the activities provided that they are related to this goal area.'*

Step 3. Planning for on-going evaluation

Review your progress and set new goals as time proceeds. For example, even if you carried out all the activities related to a particular goal area once, you might wish to do them again. Indeed, many of the activities are such that they can be incorporated into your everyday way of doing your job. Columns 5 and 7 of Table 5.3 are provided to help with this continuous process of goal setting, while columns 4 and 6 provide you with the opportunity to review your progress.

CONCLUSION

In this chapter we have described three different ways in which you can diagnose your own self-development needs and set some appropriate goals. In Part 2 we present a number of activities that will help you in achieving these goals. In Chapter 6 we give a guide to selecting activities for the development of each of the 11 qualities of the effective manager, followed by a chart which relates the activities to the particular qualities. Chapter 7 gives some general guidelines on the use of the activities, which are contained in Part 2.

*Chapter 6 provides a means of identifying which activities are related to each particular goal area.

1 Score from Table 5.2	2 Corresponding quality of effective manager	3 1st goals Today's date is ___	4 Progress review Date ___	5 2nd goals Today's date is ___	6 Progress review Date ___	7 3rd goals Today's date is ___
A:	1. Command of basic facts					
B:	2. Relevant professional knowledge and understanding					
C:	3. Continuing sensitivity to events					
D:	4. Problem-solving, analytical, and decision/judgement-making skills					
E:	5. Social skills and abilities					
F:	6. Emotional resilience					
G:	7. Proactivity— inclination to respond purposefully to events					
H:	8. Creativity					
I:	9. Mental agility					
J:	10. Balanced learning habits and skills					
K:	11. Self-knowledge					

Table 5.3. For use with self-diagnosis Method Three: self-administered questionnaire

6 A guide to the selection of activities

By now you will have set yourself some learning goals for self-development. This brief chapter is about how you select some of the 'activities' set out in the remaining part of the book.

Table 6.1 shows along the top the 11 areas of learning, and down the left-hand side the name and number of each of the 49 activities provided for you in this book. We have put a large cross in the column for each learning area against each activity which is designed to bring about *major learning* in that area. We have put small crosses where we believe that there is some payoff from the activity, although it is not primarily designed for learning in the area covered.

By going down the columns of the learning areas which are priorities for you, you can begin to choose activities which should be relevant to you.

You will need an approach to decide the order in which to tackle activities. Here are three possibilities:

1. You will remember that four of the learning areas: self-knowledge, balanced learning habits, mental agility, and creativity, are thought to be important to managers because they allow them to develop quickly and use the other more specific skills and qualities. One strategy is for you to start with any learning goals you may have in these areas, because it makes sense to start with activities which help you 'learn to learn'. This will help you get the most out of subsequent activities.
2. Another possiblity, appropriate if your time is limited or if the problems that you want to learn to cope with are pressing, is to start with your most urgent learning goals, the ones that you have concluded are your greatest area of weakness.
3. You could begin by trying one or two of the activities, and make up your mind what to do next as you go along. This will allow you to get a feel for the kind of activities that suit you. We expect that some of the activities will work for you better than others and that these will not necessarily be the same as those that work, or do not work, for other people.

Activities	Self-knowledge	Balanced learning habits	Mental agility	Creativity	Proactivity	Emotional resilience	Social skills	Analytical skill	Sensitivity to events	Professional knowledge	Situational facts
1. Extend your knowledge of situational facts									X		X
2. Making contacts					X		X				X
3. Managing your time										X	
4. Keeping up to date		X								X	
5. Facts and assumptions	X						X		X		
6. Personal journal	X	X						X	X		
7. Powerlines					X		X		X		
8. Differences and discrimination									X	X	
9. Micro-political mapping					X		X		X		
10. Credulous listening		X			X		X		X		
11. Decision making								X			
12. Planning and decision-making skills								X		X	
13. Choosing solutions with a chance								X			
14. Role set analysis								X			X
15. Planning change					X			X			
16. Analysis of experiences	X	X			X			X	X		
17. Catastrophic contingencies	X			X	X	X		X			
18. Budgetary control			X					X		X	X
19. Asserting yourself	X				X	X	X				
20. Response to conflict						X	X		X		
21. Practising new group behaviours					X		X	X	X		
22. Interpreting yourself and others	X						X	X			
23. Counselling style inventory	X						X		X		
24. Getting to know you	X						X				
25. Getting to yes						X	X		X		

Activities	Self-knowledge	Balanced learning habits	Mental agility	Creativity	Proactivity	Emotional resilience	Social skills	Analytical skill	Sensitivity to events	Professional knowledge	Situational facts
26. Collaborative working				X		X	X				
27. Looking after yourself	X				X	X					
28. Relaxation						X					
29. Fitness						X					
30. Managing your feelings	X					X	X				
31. Stability zones						X					
32. Who's the boss?					X		X	X			
33. Practising change					X	X			X		
34. Action planning			X		X			X			
35. Imaging				X	X				X		
36. Accepting other people's ideas	X			X				X			
37. Brainstorming				X					X		
38. Approaches to creativity				X							
39. Attribute alternatives				X							
40. Coping with complexity			X			X	X				
41. Quick thinking			X								
42. Developing a helicopter mind		X	X	X							
43. Managing your dependency		X									
44. Understanding your learning processes	X	X							X		
45. Study skills	X	X								X	
46. How do you learn?	X								X		
47. Mind your language	X	X					X				X
48. Conversations with yourself	X			X							
49. Backwards review	X					X			X		

Table 6.1. Activities/learning areas matrix

7 How to use the activities

One point before you start on the activities: there are many paths to self-development and the approach offered in this book is just one. Through learner control and responsibility, management self-development takes many guises. Some of those most commonly found within organizations are:

- coaching/counselling;
- appraisal;
- internal rotation, attachment, and placement;
- external attachments and placements;
- reading;
- committee membership;
- discussion groups, working parties, meetings of professional bodies and institutes;
- learning from one's own job and experience;
- special activities.

This book represents one example of the last two categories in the list. Many of the experiences listed do not lead to development or learning. They either take predictable routine courses, such as in committees or professional-body gatherings, or they are used too frequently as control rather than development mechanisms, such as in personnel appraisal. This need not be so. With effort on the part of the manager involved, most of the experiences can become enriching and rewarding. We recommend that you scan all of the self-development opportunities open to you and take advantage of some of them.

First, though, the main purpose of this book is to provide you with a number of activities or exercises which you can use as part of your self-development programme. Here are a few notes which we hope will help you to get the most out of them.

Commitment

There is no point in cheating. Just as exercises for physical fitness are of no use if you only pretend to do them, or do them halfheartedly, so with the mental exercises in this book. The more you put into them, the more you will get out of them.

Working with a partner

The activities can all be done on your own, but even more benefit can be obtained through working with a partner. It doesn't matter *who* the partner is (colleague, friend, spouse), but it is important *what* he or she is. The partner should be someone you can trust and who will help by providing you with honest feedback and by being a good, challenging listener. Ideally, each of you should undertake to help the other so that, as well as helping, each is being helped. Working with a partner can also increase commitment to the programme.

If you decide to work with a partner, 'Getting to Know You' (Activity 24) provides an opportunity to build a useful helping relationship.

Working with support groups

This involves a number—say 4 or more people—agreeing to try out the activities in their own time. At regular intervals (once or twice a month) they meet for a couple of hours to share experiences and help each other by discussion, giving feedback, and support. Your personnel or training manager might help if you want to set up such a group in your own organization. Alternatively, ask your local college or university if it will set up a support group as part of its management education programme.

When and where?

A number of the activities are such that you will have little choice of location; others can be done wherever you like.

Obviously you need a time and place where you will be free from interruption. You might like to set aside an hour at lunch-time, or in the evening. You might find it possible to do some activities on the train (instead of the crossword puzzle). It really is up to you. However, we suggest that you try to set aside certain specific periods of time, rather than just saying, 'I'll have a go when I get the chance'. Setting aside a particular time is a necessary act of commitment to the self-development programme.

Once you have started work on the activities, they will tend to become incorporated into the way you work.

Doing

Each activity is designed around a three-stage model of learning (Fig. 7.1):

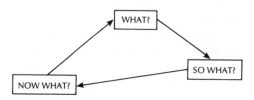

Figure 7.1. Doing the activities

The 'what?' phase

Basically, this is the experience itself, and your immediate observations. The activities tell you what to do, and ask you to note what happens. It is very important to write down your observations when instructed to do so. Writing is an aid to commitment, helps to clarify what is going on, and serves as a reference for future use.

The 'so what?' phase

This consists of thinking about what happened, and noting your reactions to it. These reactions might be feelings, ideas, insights, questions. As time goes on, you might find that at this stage you can see a link between what is happening now and what happened on a previous occasion. This link might be in similarities (of ideas, reactions, or feelings), of changes in yourself, and so on. Again, writing these down is likely to increase the benefits you will gain from the activity.

The 'now what?' phase

This is perhaps the most difficult. It consists of taking stock of what you have done and what you have observed, felt, and learned (the 'what?' and 'so what?'), and deciding its significance for you in future action. Thus the 'now what?' phase requires you to make concrete plans for future behaviour based on the insights and developments that the exercise has given you. It is particularly important to try to write these down, since they can then be used as the basis for on-going personal evaluation.

Incorporation of activities into everyday behaviour

We do not claim that doing each of these activities once will develop you into a perfect manager. Rather, the idea is that by doing the exercises you will start the process of examining yourself in light of the 11 qualities of an effective manager, and start a development process which, if continued, will have considerable effect.

Therefore, the aim is to incorporate the ways of behaviour that are established by the activities into your everyday behaviour. You might do this by repeating an activity, possibly with modifications to suit your circumstances. When you have done this a few times, particularly if you notice the various skills and abilities growing as you do so, you should make a conscious effort to turn everyday situations into activities for self-development.

As time goes on, then, you will, we hope, be keeping track of your own progress (Chapter 5 gives some ways of doing this; also Activity 6, 'Personal Journal', can serve this purpose), repeating activities, modifying them, generating your own, and gradually using your own everyday work experiences as opportunities for experimentation, learning, and self-development. When you reach this stage, you will be what someone once called a 'learning manager', and this book will have achieved its purpose.

Part 2
Activities for management self-development

Part 2 consists entirely of 49 self-development activities numbered and in the order given in Table 6.1. As we mentioned earlier, the sequence is not designed to lead you through from 1 to 49. To get the most out of the exercises you need to develop a learning strategy along the lines suggested in Chapter 6.

Although the activities are designed as self-contained units to stand alone or in sequence with others, there is inevitably some overlap. This occurs where it is necessary for the completeness of one particular activity. This has been kept to a minimum, but you will come across some repetition.

To summarize briefly, you can work through the activities:

- alone
- with a partner
- in a small self-development group

depending upon your situation and your preferred learning style. The extent to which you are able to transfer learning into your job behaviour will depend upon a number of variables other than your own skills and abilities. For example, it depends upon the extent to which you are allowed to try out new ideas by your boss and those in senior positions. It depends on the extent to which your organization encourages new ideas and initiatives. It also depends upon the learning climate of your organization.

One final reminder, you are almost certainly someone else's boss. This puts you in a strong position to help and influence the learning and development of your staff. How well are you cultivating a good learning climate?

Activity 1
Extend your knowledge of situational facts

LEARNING AREAS: SITUATIONAL FACTS: Sensitivity to events

All the time at work you make decisions and put them into practice. Decisions take facts into account. Facts are an input to a decision. However good your decision-making abilities, your decisions and the actions which follow them will be wrong if they are based on inaccurate information. We distinguish here between situational and professional facts. Situational facts are things like the price of a commodity, the size of an order book, a customer's delivery deadline. Professional facts are to do with the technology of a production process, or a specialist management area like industrial relations legislation, or financial reporting requirements.

Professional facts are distinct from professional skills and procedures. They are the professional inputs to *managerial* rather than *professional* decisions. The manager of a plant with a sophisticated technology may have a technical background sufficient to make *managerial* decisions; to plan, for instance, the plant's output and manning, taking account of the need for maintenance. If the plant breaks down technically, the manager may choose to get involved in the technical/professional search for a solution, but this is temporarily giving up management and returning to a technical/professional role.

Here we are concerned with professional facts as inputs to managerial decisions, rather than with professional skills in dealing with professional problems.

Situational and professional facts vary in their permanence, from highly variable—like the price of raw materials and the stock level of finished goods—to relatively permanent ones like the date of annual stocktaking, or the order pattern of a regular customer.

Reviewing your command of situational and professional facts

The problem in developing your command of situational and professional facts is likely to be more to do with identifying what you

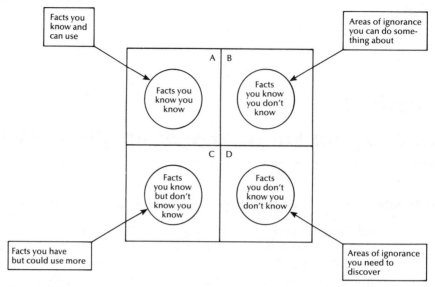

Figure A1.1

need to know than actually getting it. Indeed, once you have identified what you need to know it is probably quite easy to get it. The problem is that, usually, we don't know what we don't know and it is the data in this blind spot that we may really need. Look at the situation as shown in Fig. A1.1.

What you need to do is to convert Cs into As, Ds into Bs, and Bs into As.

To help with this, we suggest the exercise below which should help you to clarify what you already have in 'A' and 'B', add to it from 'C', and help you explore 'D'.

Activity

Step 1

Imagine that someone wants to find out whether you are really on the ball on the situational and professional facts concerning your job or occupation. Take a piece of paper and write down as many key questions about such facts of your job as it exists now, and the answers to these questions. Imagine that you have the job of compiling the test questions for a *Mastermind* or *Brain of Britain* TV or radio programme, with your job as the topic.

Step 2

Now extend the list of questions and answers by any or all of the following:

(a) If you redesigned, developed, or extended your job in any way that you think desirable, what would this add to the list of questions and answers?

(b) What are the next possible moves in your career—what new facts would you need to have at your command to perform these future jobs?

(c) What kind of training and education are provided for people coming into your kind of work, and your organization? What facts do they have that you haven't?

(d) Imagine showing your list to:
  (i) your boss;
  (ii) your staff;
  (iii) your colleagues;
  (iv) others in similar jobs to yourself;
  (v) anyone else with whom you are regularly in contact.
  What do you think they might suggest that you add to the list?

(e) Show your list to some of the people mentioned in (d) and ask them. Exchange lists with someone in a similar job to yourself who has done this exercise and discuss them both.

(Because of the 'don't-know-what-you-don't-know' factor, second opinions greatly enhance the benefit you can get from this activity. For this reason (e) is particularly important.)

FOLLOW-UP

You probably know the answers to most of the new questions you have posed, but make a list of things you need to know about the others. If any of them are difficult, other activities related to the learning areas 'Sensitivity to Events' and 'Balanced Learning Habits' (Table 6.1) will help you.

Activity 2
Making contacts

LEARNING AREAS: SITUATIONAL FACTS: Social skills: Proactivity

The effective manager knows not only 'what's what', but also 'who's who'. To be effective we need a lot of contacts within the organization; we need to know what others do, how they can help us, and how we can help them.

The activity

The first step is to decide whom you are going to get to know. There are a number of ways of doing this, including the following:

1. Look at an organization chart and choose people in areas about which you know very little.
2. Use an internal telephone directory to the same end.
3. Choose people in offices around you.
4. Choose people whom you have seen about the place, without knowing who they are, what they do.
5. Choose people at random, the third person who enters a lift or walks into the canteen; stick a pin into the internal telephone book.

Having chosen your first potential contact, get to know him or her. This will be more difficult than it sounds, but less difficult than you imagine. You can explain frankly that you are trying to get to know more people, or, if you prefer a more furtive approach, just try to engage the chosen person in informal conversation.

We suggest that your goal should be to find answers to at least the following questions:

(a) What is the person's name?
(b) What is his or her job title?
(c) What does that job involve?
(d) How does this person see the main purpose of the job and its contribution to the organization? Do you agree? If not, can you explore this difference?
    you

1. If you want fairly long, descriptive answers, ask open-ended questions, such as:

   'What . . .?'
   'How do you . . .?'
   'Could you explain . . .?'
   'Can you give an example of . . .?'
   'How do you feel about . . .?'
   'Why do you . . .?'

2. Unless you want very specific, precise, short answers, avoid closed questions, such as:

   'Do you . . .?'
   'How often . . .?'
   'Is it true that . . .?'
   'How many . . .?'

3. Notice non-verbal cues, such as tone of voice, changes in posture, facial expression, eye movement, gestures, speech hesitancies.

4. Respond to non-verbal cues by using them to suggest further questions, by remarking on them, or by changing the subject, whichever you think most appropriate.

5. Check out and clarify what you are hearing; that is, repeat in your own words what you think the other person has said, what is meant, and how he or she feels.

6. If the other person talks mostly about feelings, it might be useful to ask about ideas or facts; on the other hand, if facts are offered at the time, then try asking about feelings.

7. From time to time, find out the other person's feelings about you and the process of the discussion.

8. All the time, ask yourself if you are prepared to be as open with the other as you are asking him or her to be with you.

Table A2.1. Hints on getting another person to talk freely

(e) What are his or her major goals, concerns, issues, problems?
(f) In what way can the person be of help to you?
(g) In what way can you be of help to him or her?
(h) Are there any ways in which the person's goals, needs, or interests conflict with yours? If so, what can be done to lessen or overcome this conflict?

You will need to develop certain skills to get the person talking about these things. Some hints on how to do this are given in Table A2.1.

FOLLOW-UP

As time goes on you should, using this approach, gradually build an excellent network of contacts throughout the organization. This network will enable you to keep tuned in to what's going on. It will provide you with sources of information, help, and support when needed. In turn, you will be helping others when they need you.

Networking is one of the new arts of managing. Basically you have to devote time to going around and talking to the right people, which has always been the case but is now even more vital in the 'age of information'. 'Corporate networking: how to tap unconventional wisdom' by Robert Mueller and 'IT in the 1990s: managing organisational interdependence' by John Rockart and James Short are Chapters 12 and 23 in Jane Henry's (ed.) *Creative Management* (Sage and Open University, 1991). *The New Organization: Growing the Culture of Organizational Networking* by Colin Hastings (McGraw-Hill, 1993) shows how sharing know-how through organizational and interorganizational networking breaks down communications blocks and builds up flexibility.

Activity 3

Managing your time

LEARNING AREAS: PROFESSIONAL KNOWLEDGE: Situational facts: Analytical skills

When most of us think of scarcity, we think of economic scarcity—which Marx blamed for the division of industrial society into classes and which caused Keynes to speculate that if the economic problem were solved, people would be deprived of their traditional purpose. Perhaps scarcity will never disappear, but old scarcities will be replaced by new ones. New scarcities, like fresh air, open space, and pure water, appear as industry expands to remove the old scarcities. A major scarcity for us in the late twentieth century is time. We will have to budget time as we have budgeted money in the past. There are many reasons for this. In industrial societies, a common characteristic is the careful measurement and allocation of work, but an increasingly common feature is the careful measurement and calculation of leisure time. We have time-saving devices, which paradoxically demand time for maintenance, along with our greatly increased stock of consumer goods. Time is required for our greatly increased capacity to consume and the opportunities for time spending become richer every year. We calculate the opportunity cost of spending time even with friends, relatives, and loved ones.

Make a quick inventory of your free time for the rest of the week:

Hours

Monday

Tuesday

Wednesday

Thursday

63

Friday

Saturday

Sunday

Note down for each day how much free time you have. What is left after sleeping, eating, working, travelling? Then try putting down things you could do in this time, under three headings:

1. Things I MUST do this week.
2. Things I SHOULD do this week.
3. Things I would LIKE to do this week (if only I had the time).

As this is a private list and for your eyes only, you can afford to be honest with yourself. For example, have you included time for being with close friends and family? Time for doing nothing much? Time to recover from doing too much? Time for passing the time of day with all those other faces and acquaintances in your life?

Peter Drucker once pointed out how valuable is this 'free' time— 'discretionary time is one of the scarcest and most precious of commodities'. We know the truth of Parkinson's first law: 'Work expands to fill the time available for its completion'. The activity in this section is designed to help you look at how you spend your time at work—although you may wish also to look at how you spend your time out of work. We are concerned primarily with managerial effectiveness and if you feel your outside-work activity is relevant to your job, look at that part of your life too.

A main purpose of the activity is to gain some feeling of control over how your time is spent. This might involve cutting out unnecessary or unrewarding chunks of time but it might also include looking for chunks of time in which to do things which you're not doing at the moment but which you ought or would like to be doing.

For example, a manager in a large retail company looked at the way she used working time. She discovered that she spent *three hours every day* overseeing and checking the work of her staff (and another hour each day eating lunch). On top of her own busy job she had staff members who didn't accept responsibility and who did not exercise initiative. She had a weight problem, because she never had enough time to take exercise. What she could not see was that the way she spent time was linked to her other problems. How could members of staff exercise responsibility if she gave them no discretion—if their work was continuously checked? She could have gained another half hour by having a light lunch and a walk instead of her usual one-hour three-courser in the management dining room.

So, managing your time properly may increase others' effectiveness and capacity as well as your own. It is also one of the keys to the thorny problem of delegation—are you spending your time on the right activities? We can see you're busy—but doing what?

Managing time is one aspect of managing yourself. One of our characteristics of the effective manager is proactivity: being a self-starter, taking personal responsibility, and getting something done. You can start here.

Activity

1. *Recording* how your time is spent.
2. *Analysing* on what you spend your time.
3. *Making decisions* about the most effective use of your discretionary time.

Step 1

Before you can manage your time you need to find out what you're doing with it.

Record your activities at work for the next five days. You can design your own recording sheet or use the one given in Table A3.1.

Spend five days *at least*, on this—the full value of the exercise cannot be gained from less.

Step 2

Analyse your data sheets under a number of headings.

(a) OUTCOME
How successful were the various activities?
Have you any habitual failures?

(b) TYPE OF WORK
Divide your work tasks into three categories:

  (i) Things you MUST do?—Your most important duties.
 (ii) Things you SHOULD do?—Your next most important duties.
(iii) Things you would LIKE to do?—Your least important duties.

TIME LOG

Day: _____ Date: _____

Describe WHAT HAPPENS in detail—the subject of meetings, phone calls, letters, reading, conversations. Note the DURATION of each happening. Note the NAME and POSITION of OTHER PEOPLE INVOLVED. Include even casual encounters.

Time	What happened?	Duration	People involved	Comments
9.00 9.30				
9.30 10.00				
10.00 10.30				
10.30 11.00				
11.00 11.30				
11.30 12.00				
12.00 12.30				
12.30 1.00				
1.00 1.30				
1.30 2.00				
2.00 2.30				
2.30 3.00				
3.00 3.30				
3.30 4.00				
4.00 4.30				
4.30 5.00				
5.00 5.30				

Table A3.1

Allocate a theoretical percentage of your effort to each of these, e.g.:

  (i) 75 per cent.
 (ii) 20 per cent.
(iii) 5 per cent.

How much of your time are you spending on each set of activities compared to the 'correct' theoretical mix?

We often concentrate on things we are able to do or like doing at the expense of things which we find difficult. These difficult tasks may be the most vital ones.

Another way of looking at this is to ask yourself what proportion of my time goes on:

  (i) MANAGERIAL WORK—i.e., planning, organizing, motivating.
 (ii) PROFESSIONAL SKILLS—i.e., exercising your old specialist professional skills.

Another common trap is the carrying over of professional work from one's original occupation, e.g., sales, engineering, accounting, into the manager's job. Of course you need to exercise these skills part of the time, but exactly how much is appropriate:

10 per cent?
15 per cent?
20 per cent?

And how much are you *actually* doing?

The *managerial* work may be the most difficult and you may be avoiding it—preferring the comfort of working in your old craft or field.

(c) WHERE DOES THE WORK COME FROM?

  (i) Boss—is the boss delegating enough?
         —is the boss using you as a personal assistant?
 (ii) Staff—are they too dependent upon you?
(iii) Self—are you setting yourself enough tasks?
(iv) Elsewhere—where?
         —how important are these?

(d) DELEGATION
For each task/happening ask yourself:

  (i) Could this have been delegated?
 (ii) If YES, to whom?
    If NO, why not?—your answer to this one should be really thoughtful.

—Is it really your job or have you made yourself indispensable?

You may be able to think of some more headings under which you
can analyse your time log.

Step 3

After analysis it's time to make some decisions about how to spend
your time.

(a) WHAT THINGS ARE YOU SPENDING TIME ON THAT YOU
COULD EITHER CUT OUT, CUT DOWN, OR DELEGATE?
(b) WHAT THINGS ARE YOU NOT DOING NOW THAT YOU
SHOULD BE—OR WHAT THINGS SHOULD YOU BE DOING
MORE OF?
You can use your three job areas:
(i) MUST do
(ii) SHOULD do
(iii) would LIKE to do
Make sure the MUST DOs are done!
(c) WHAT ACTIONS WILL YOU COMMIT YOURSELF TO HERE AND
NOW?

	Action	*Completed by:*
1.		
2.		
3.		
4.		
etc.		

FOLLOW-UP

Obviously you can repeat your time log any time you like to check
out how you're functioning, when your best times are, and so on.

Over the last 20 or 30 years much research has looked at how
managers actually spend their time. If you're interested in reading
about this, Henry Mintzberg's *The Nature of Managerial Work*
(Harper and Row, 1973) and John Kotter's *The General Managers*
(The Free Press, 1982) are good sources. There are numerous self-
help books on time management. Sally Garratt's *Manage Your Time*
(Fontana, 1985) is full of practical tips and assessment activities.
Lester Bittel's *Right on Time!* (McGraw-Hill, 1991) takes a broader
view in looking at managing not only your own time, but also that of
others and the organization as a whole.

Activity 4
Keeping up to date

Successful managers know what is going on. Skill and judgement need to rest upon a base of up-to-date professional knowledge. A good manager needs to know about new developments in terms of specialist expertise and, more generally, in terms of changes in markets, legislation, culture, fashions, and so on.

The purpose of this activity is to encourage you to think about your personal strategy for keeping up to date and to suggest some ways of doing this.

Activity

Step 1

First, here are some questions to answer. Take your time and think about them before you answer.

(a) How much time do you spend READING in your field each week?

(b) How would you describe the way you read this material (e.g., scanning, gleaning, immersing yourself, etc.)?

(c) Write down the names of the JOURNALS, MAGAZINES or NEWSLETTERS that you read regularly in your field.

(d) Which relevant JOURNALS, MAGAZINES or NEWSLETTERS do you *not* see or read?

(e) Do you ever make use of TRAINING PACKAGES, that is, manuals, interactive videos, computer-based learning or programmed approaches to learning?

(f) Do you ever make use of CORRESPONDENCE COURSES or DISTANCE LEARNING?

(g) Write down the names of the PROFESSIONAL BODIES or ASSOCIATIONS to which you belong.

(h) Write down which COURSES and CONFERENCES you have attended in the last year.

(i) Have you made any VISITS or STUDY TOURS in the last year?

(j) What other ways of developing your professional knowledge have you used in the last year?

Step 2

Now look over your answers to these ten questions. What sort of a picture do you get? Does continuing professional development end up at the bottom of your pile of priorities or are you taking it seriously? Do you have a strategy for the future?

Neglecting keeping up to date can happen easily because it is not a 'crisis' issue. Its effects are cumulative, insidious over time, the error realized only several years later. Putting time into your continuing professional development is like investing in a business— there will be few benefits tomorrow without investments in people, plant, and products today. Or, if you prefer a more homely example, you can't expect a good crop of beans without a generous investment of manure.

Now let's examine your answers in more detail. Many of them concern the activity of reading and even now in this TV age this is an essential part of keeping up to date for most of us. You wouldn't have got this far (as a manager or in this book!) without reading. One way to make sure that we do enough reading and gain most benefit from it is to read *purposefully*. (We are talking here, of course, in the context of professional knowledge, and not of reading as 'just' a pastime, or 'just' for pleasure. Some of us who need to read a lot in our jobs do have another problem of sometimes being unable to read slowly or purely for pleasure. But here we are dealing with more the problem of not reading enough or effectively.)

Step 3

Choose something to read—a paper, article, chapter of a book. Find a time and place when you can sit down and read it. Now review your reading with the aid of the questions in Table A4.1. We have given some sample answers here, but make sure you provide your own.

Reviewing your reading will give you an insight into how you go about it. For example:

Reading review questions	*Some sample answers*
1. For how long did I read?	e.g.,—for five minutes, then I was interrupted — for half an hour, then I became bored — for ten minutes until I became exasperated with the author's views
2. Did I skim or jump forwards?	e.g.,—No. I plodded through —Yes. I skimmed it first —Yes, because I couldn't understand that bit or because I knew that bit
3. Did I go back to re-read bits?	e.g.,—Yes. I re-read when I couldn't understand — No. I just kept going through —Yes, because a later bit reminded me of an earlier bit so I checked back
4. Did I pause at all?	e.g.,—Yes. I needed to think about an idea I had while reading —Yes. I needed a break —No. I made myself go on through
5. Did I take notes?	e.g.,—Yes. Just main headings and definitions —No. I don't need to remember any of this —Yes. It's just habit with me
6. What was my purpose in reading?	e.g.,—to extract practical ideas —to check my level of understanding in this field —to memorize for an examination —to decide whether to buy or borrow it

Table A4.1

- *Why* do you read (and why *don't* you)? (To glean or ransack; to escape; to meditate on, etc.)
- *When* do you read? (What's the best time and place for you?)
- *What* do you do when you get bored, lose the thread or disagree with what's written? (Give up; take a break; get angry; eat a sandwich, etc.)
- For *how long* can you/do you read?

Getting better at understanding you and your reading habits makes it more likely that you will know when it is best to read what sort of material for what purpose. We all have our own patterns and preferences which we need to be aware of to get the best out of our reading.

Step 4

Now choose another paper or book chapter. Find time and space to read it. Before you start, note down the following:

- Your purpose in reading this.
- How much time you have for reading.
- Whether or not you will take notes.
- Whether or not you will skim it first.
- Where you will do your reading.
- What you will do when you get bored/frustrated, etc.

Now read. Now take the time to review again using questions in Step 3. Are your patterns becoming clearer?

Step 5

Our original questions in Step 1 (c) and (d) were about JOURNALS, MAGAZINES, and NEWSLETTERS, all of which obviously involve reading and which are an important source of up-to-date knowledge. Journal and magazine articles often lead books by several years in terms of new fields of knowledge being opened up.

Take the lists you made in Step 1 (c) and (d) to your librarian or to a knowledgeable friend. (If you haven't got either of these, that tells you something about your keeping up-to-date strategy—perhaps a first step would be to find one?) Ask your librarian or friend to check your lists and to add to your question (d) list if possible. Is there any comment on your choices? What does he or she read? Can you be put on a 'circulation list' for any recommended journals? And so on. There are often plenty of journals, newsletters, etc., around which don't get read by many people through not being circulated properly. In this way you can begin to build up a circulating network or 'papernet' where you swop items of mutual interest with professional colleagues.

Step 6

Questions (e) and (f) ask about your use of TRAINING PACKAGES and DISTANCE LEARNING. There are an increasing number of these now being made available for busy managers who have only odd spaces and times for study. If you are fortunate enough to work in an organization with a training department, then this is the place to start. Make demands on your training person—that's what he or she is there for. Otherwise your librarian again will be a key contact; but you can also try the local college, polytechnic or university where there may be 'learning resources centres'. Relevant professional associations are also a good source of information. You can contact them for lists of relevant packages and resources. For example, the BIM (British Institute of Management) has an excellent education information unit which will answer queries about all sorts of professional development activities.

Step 7

Question (g) asks about membership of PROFESSIONAL BODIES and ASSOCIATIONS. This is often an excellent way of keeping up to date. Professional bodies not only often have conferences and branch meetings where you can meet other members, but also circulate newsletters and journals. Again, if you don't know which ones might be relevant for you, you can find out from the same sources as listed under Step 6.

Step 8

COURSES, CONFERENCES and VISITS are another way of updating and learning. Is it really impossible for you to find the time and money to spend two or three days per year doing this? If you really don't have these opportunities, how are you compensating for that? (Courses, of course, are the commonest way of keeping up to date. They often prove not to be developmental because they are not designed specifically for you, and because people get sent on them rather than choosing them for themselves. Therefore, make sure you choose yourself, and carefully, and know why you're going.)

Step 9

Have you any other ideas for keeping up to date? Perhaps some of the methods in this activity are not open to you. One way to generate some new thoughts is to go round and informally circulate your colleagues—how do they keep themselves up to date?

Step 10

A strategy for keeping up to date. After considering all these methods how are you going to ensure you stay up to date? It is best to have a strategy which has two parts:

(a) *Choose* which methods of keeping up to date you will follow in the next, say, six months.
(b) *Plan* when, where, how, you will do these chosen activities. Use a table like that in Activity 34 'Action Planning', to help you do this and commit yourself to goals, target dates, etc. It is also a good idea to find a colleague, confederate or confidant with whom you can share your plan, discuss it, and review progress from time to time. This helps a lot.

FOLLOW-UP

More detailed advice on these various ways to keep yourself up to date can be found in Tom Boydell's *Management Self-development: A Handbook for Managers, Organisations and Institutions* (International Labour Office, Geneva, 1985). *Key Business Concepts* by Bengt Karloff (Routledge, 1993) is an alphabetical guide to 50 modern management concepts together with explanations of 20 well-known management models. *The Manager's Handbook: The Practical Guide to Successful Management*, written by staff from Arthur Young (Sphere, 1986), is a short, well-illustrated tour of many aspects of management and organizations.

Activity 5
Facts and assumptions

LEARNING AREAS: SENSITIVITY TO EVENTS: Self-knowledge: Social skills

In life we do not often bother to separate out facts from assumptions. We do not have the time. When I enter my office in the morning, I observe facts and make assumptions. I observe that the office door is shut, but I assume much more: that the room has been cleaned; that the papers I left on my desk last night are still there; that the furniture is arranged as I left it; and so on. When I go to a meeting, I observe that certain people are present, but I make assumptions: how certain individuals will behave; how long the meeting will last; whether I will be interested or bored; and so on.

Assumptions nearly always outweigh observations, and this ability to assume, i.e., to predict, is a valuable human skill, without which progress and behaviour would be painfully slow and limited. However, there are a number of times when I make wrong assumptions: that my office has been cleaned when it hasn't, or that so-and-so will talk all the time and he or she is silent. Sometimes all this causes is surprise, but sometimes action is based on a false assumption. If I thought so-and-so would attack my ideas at the meeting I might decide attack was the best form of defence and attack first. When I am attacked back my assumption is confirmed. Or is it? Would he or she have attacked if I had not? This is a self-fulfilling prophecy—when I make an assumption; act on that assumption; and my action causes another to act in a way which confirms my original but false assumption.

Another pitfall is that I may not observe certain facts if I have already made assumptions which are contrary to those facts. If I assume that so-and-so is going to attack me, I only see the aggression and, if I notice friendly acts, interpret them as 'softening-up' tactics. This is 'selective perception'. I see what I want to see; select those things I am looking for. One goes into a room looking for a book and does not notice a new furniture arrangement, because one is not looking for it. There is a danger in operating on untested assumptions and perceiving selectively from the environment.

This activity is designed to help build those mental muscles which distinguish 'facts' from 'assumptions'.

The activity

Step 1

Choose a relative stranger who has either recently joined your organization, or whom you have only recently come across.

Step 2

Observe the person closely and make a list of all those things which you can verify as facts: dress, appearance, expressions, behaviour. Philosophically, it is perhaps impossible to justify anything as a fact, but there are some things about which we can be relatively certain: 'He is very tall' (of a 6′ 3″ man), for instance. But how factual is the statement 'She is very nice'? Even 'very tall' is subjective and may not be regarded as fact when talking about a 6′ 3″ basketball player. The safest rule is to ask yourself: 'What will I accept as a fact, that is a given or commonly verifiable piece of information, in this particular situation?'

Step 3

Now make another list, this time of assumptions. These may be based upon the facts you have observed, but they should be assumptions, guesses, or predictions arising out of those facts on such matters as status, religion, likes or dislikes, personality problems, marital status, habits, opinions, attitudes, and so on.

Some of these assumptions may be relatively safe: it is a fact that she is tall, therefore it is fair to assume that 'she finds the office desks uncomfortable to sit at'. Or they might be more 'risky'. 'She is tall', therefore can one assume 'her husband is tall also', or 'she feels embarrassed at being so tall'? Be honest with yourself and list all the assumptions that come to mind.

Step 4

When you have made your list of assumptions, estimate how many will be correct. If possible, check these out with the person, explaining the object of the exercise. Whatever happens you will have made a new acquaintance and possibly a friend!

What proportion of your assumptions were correct?

(If you can't pluck up the courage to approach the person in question, you could ask a friend or colleague to go through the same activity and compare lists. What did you observe that your friend did not? and vice versa? What assumptions did each of you make?)

FOLLOW-UP

1. *Questions to ponder*

(a) What did you learn about the nature of 'facts'?

(b) What did you learn about the number of assumptions you habitually make about people and situations?

(c) Did you discover how selective your perception is?

(d) Can you think of other situations at work where you go through similar facts—assumptions, connections?

2. *Further reading*

If you're interested in the questions of perception of others and the problem of discerning what you will accept as 'facts' and what are more clearly 'assumptions', any general social psychology text should have relevant reading under the heading of 'perception' or 'person perception'.

Facts by Bede Rundle is a short book of accessible philosophy on the issues surrounding the nature of facts and values (Duckworth, 1993). The view that our world is 'socially constructed' has gained ground in recent years and is particularly relevant to life in organizations. Peter Berger and Thomas Luckman's *the Social Construction of Reality* (Penguin, 1991) has acquired classic status since its first appearance in 1966. This or Anthony Giddens' *New Rules of Sociological Method* (Polity Press, 2nd edn, 1993) will really get you into the issues.

3. *Further activity*

(a) If you'd like to see how your skills are developing, repeat the activity with the next suitable person, or . . .

(b) Try a variation at the next meeting or interview you attend. Draw up lists of 'facts' and 'assumptions' beforehand or at the very beginning. Observe during the event and check back on your lists afterwards. If you do this once or twice, you might be surprised at (i) how observant you're becoming; (ii) how accurate your assumptions are becoming; (iii) how cautious you are now about making assumptions!

Activity 6
Personal journal

LEARNING AREAS: SENSITIVITY TO EVENTS: Analytical skills: Self-knowledge: Balanced learning habits

The underlying theme running throughout this book is the value of reflecting upon one's own behaviour. If you can do this in a purposeful, insightful manner, you will become more able to tune in to situations and to learn from experiences, and will develop a greater self-awareness and ability to cope with pressure and emotions.

To gain maximum benefit from many of the activities, they should be repeated several times, particularly this one. It is necessary to keep the journal over a period of weeks or even months to get the most out of it.

There is nothing new in the idea of keeping some form of diary. However, to help make such an exercise more meaningful for self-development, this form of personal journal is structured around a simple model of an individual's behaviour in a particular situation.

According to this model, there are three aspects of behaviour:

1. The individual's FEELINGS: the way a person behaves is very much determined by his or her feelings in a given situation. We are often unaware—or at best only half aware—of the nature of our feelings and the effect they are having. In our society there is a tendency to suppress or deny feelings—'the stiff upper lip' is still admired—but if you are to be in control of your behaviour, it is essential to be sensitive to your feelings and their effects.

2. The individual's THOUGHTS and IDEAS: in any situation the individual lives through a number of thoughts and ideas. Important among these are the factors perceived in a situation and ideas about courses of action. These will depend on the various elements of the current situation and will be influenced by the individual's assumptions and the perceptions brought in from previous experience.

Also important will be the new thoughts and ideas that are triggered off by the new situation.

3. The individual's ACTION-TENDENCIES: The individual will have various action-tendencies: predispositions to certain types of action. For example, in committee and disagreeing strongly with the views of the chairperson, we may nonetheless say nothing because we are scared of challenging authority. This fear, or lack of self-confidence, will result in an action-tendency of saying/doing nothing. Another action-tendency could be described as precipitous: a strong need to *do* something rather than to think things out carefully—a tendency which leads to over-hasty action.

Action-tendencies are internal motivations or forces that push individuals towards certain types of action or inaction.

These three elements each influence the individual's action behaviour. Take the example of a manager in committee. The chairperson seems to be supporting something with which I, the manager, disagree. My *thoughts/ideas* are that what has been said is wrong. As a result, my *feelings* are those of concern and excitement. However, due to my *parallel feeling* of fear of ridicule, or fear of challenging authority, my *action-tendency* is to say nothing.

My behaviour in this situation will depend on which of the three elements wins out. Will my ideas and half of my feelings overcome my action-tendency, leading to my making a soundly presented contribution? Or will my other feelings combine with my negative action-tendencies, leading me to remain silent? Or again, perhaps my feelings and action-tendencies will result in my making a fumbling, incoherent statement—i.e., preventing my beautifully logical ideas from getting a fair hearing.

The elements depend on each other. For example, my thoughts as ideas about what is being said may well depend on my feelings about the person saying it—and vice versa. We can see that this model of behaviour, although simple, represents a very complicated situation. This can be shown in a diagram (Fig. A6.1), emphasizing the links between thoughts/ideas, feelings, and action-tendencies.

Feelings, thoughts/ideas, and action-tendencies don't exist in a vacuum. They arise in response to some situational stimulus (in itself affected by previous events). They result in behaviour, which leads to a new situation; and so on (see Fig. A6.2).

This is a model around which a 'Personal Journal' is based.

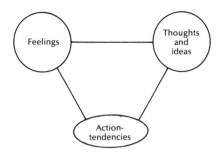

Figure A6.1

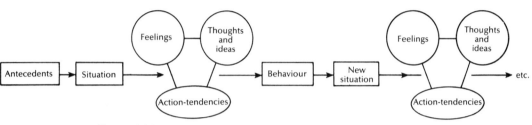

Figure A6.2

The activity

This is carried out over a period of time, and you may find it so useful that it will become established as part of your way of life— something you do all the time. Failing that, you will at least develop a 'mental' personal journal as a permanent way of thinking.

In any case, keep the journal going for a minimum of 20 entries, with at least 4 entries each week. A single entry might cover one specific incident, or may deal with a whole day's activities.

As with physical exercise, it is important to build up performance gradually, and so the activity is presented in three steps of increasing complexity.

Step 1

Take an exercise book and mark left- and right-hand pages as shown in Table A6.1.

Obviously this is only a rough guide; if you want more space under any or all of the headings, continue overleaf.

Write, on the left-hand page, a brief description of a happening. This should be factual and objective, and it is useful to include a

WHAT HAPPENED	MY RESPONSES
	My feelings
	My thoughts and ideas
	My action-tendencies
	hence
	My behaviour

Table A6.1

description of the antecedents and context—i.e., what led up to the situation.

Write down your responses to the situation on the right-hand page. Your feelings might have changed during the course of the happening. Identify and note such changes. Look for feelings that were closely followed by different ones. (For example, anger often follows a feeling of being threatened.) Note the thoughts/ideas which came into your mind during the situation; distinguish between facts and assumptions. Then note down your action-tendencies. What other factors influenced your action (or non-action). Try to identify ways in which feelings, thoughts, and action-tendencies affect each other. Finally, note down the effect of these elements on your behaviour—what did you actually do? This may have led to another situation, which can form another journal entry.

Step 2

After seven or eight entries, move on to the second phase. Complete the exercise as in Step 1, but then go on to evaluate your behaviour by recording under a new heading, 'Self-Evaluation', how you feel about your feelings, thoughts/ideas, action-tendencies, and behaviour. Do you feel good, bad, happy, sad, adequate, inadequate, guilty, disappointed, frustrated, etc.? Try to explore these self-evaluations—what do they tell you about yourself?

Step 3

After seven or eight entries at Step 2, take the journal further by adding, in the next series, another heading—'Learning'. Record what you feel you have learned from the happenings—from your feelings, thoughts/ideas, action-tendencies, behaviour, and self-evaluation.

Look back over previous journal entries, to see if patterns emerge that tell you something of significance about yourself, other people, situations, and so on.

Now write the words NOW WHAT? And try the hardest part of all. Set yourself concrete goals for behaviour that will use in a significant way the new insights and learning that you have derived from the whole exercise.

FOLLOW-UP

By compiling the journal over a period of time you should become more insightful about situations and your behaviour in them, and you will learn how to learn from everyday experience.

Activity 7
Powerlines

LEARNING AREAS: SENSITIVITY TO EVENTS: Social skills: Proactivity

If the road to hell is paved with good intentions, then efforts to change often founder on the power dynamics of the organization. We often complain about 'politics'—that something has happened for political reasons. The implication is that various influences have been exerted, negotiations have taken place—often in private—and, generally, that strings have been pulled in a way which defeats the logical, technically rational or common sense way forward.

From one perspective, organizations are political systems and managers are political actors involved in the 'art of the possible'. Effective managers need awareness, understanding and the ability to act in this world. This activity is designed to help you think about the different kinds of power around you and the various patterns of power relationships.

Sources of power in organizations

Power is a loose, hard-to-define term which includes personal attributes, resources, influences, and authority. Here are some sources of power, but this list is not exhaustive, so you might like to add some categories of your own.

(i) *Positional*—formal, hierarchical, and status-related; position power exists when one person is 'higher' than another in some structure. Such power may carry outward signs or trappings such as expensive clothes, high salaries, designated parking spaces, etc.
(ii) *Resources and rewards*—control of finance and other valued resources, access to premises and equipment and, especially, to people and information are often crucial in getting things done.
(iii) *Knowledge and expertise*—possessing technical ability or professional knowledge, such as that of accountants, maintenance engineers, chemists, doctors, lawyers, computer engineers, is increasingly vital in this 'information age'. As with resource power, such power is easily withheld and may be used to counter positional power.

(iv) *Personal influence*—including track record and prior achievements, influence is exercised in a myriad of ways, though interpersonal skills, persuasiveness, plausibility, charm, sexual
attractiveness, intellectual weight or the capacity to inspire confidence and build trust.

(v) *Networks and gossip*—with internal and external networks.
'Soft' gossipy information is often vital in terms of tip-offs about
goings-on in the organization or the outside world. Some companies run 'soft information sessions' which link with developing
environmental sensitivity and cultural awareness. The dark side of
gossip is well understood—for example, where knowledge of
someone's personal life is used to damage them—but the importance of the light side is less recognized.

(vi) *Energy and stamina*—are two important qualities in getting
things done. Many of those we dub 'great' have both of these.
Staying power through stamina, adaptability, survival skills,
occasional courage, steadfastness, standing by colleagues, persis-
tence without becoming obsessive, is often underestimated, but
frequently triumphs in the long run.

The activity

Use the matrix below to see where the power lies in your
organization—and where you stand in relation to the various kinds

Powerlines Matrix

People / Sources of power	Me	My boss	My staff	Colleagues	etc.
Positional					
Resources and rewards					
Knowledge and expertise					
Personal influence					
Networks and gossip					
Energy and stamina					
(Add your own)					

Table A7.1

of power—and at the same time carry out a quick 'power audit' of the organization.

Step 1

Think about the kinds of power outlined above and add any others which you think we have missed or which carry special importance where you work.

Step 2

Choose a current issue or project which you are thinking about or working on. For example, it might be your chances of being chosen to lead a particular new scheme, or it might be the general influence of your department compared with others. It helps your analysis of the situation if you think about power in relation to something specific.

Now, score yourself on each type of power, using the following scale:

5 = Very strong. Well placed to deal with challenge/change/competition.
4 = Strong. Able to respond to new developments.
3 = Adequate. Will get by with a fair wind and stable conditions.
2 = Weak. Not well placed to cope with new developments.
1 = Very weak. Unable to cope with what's happening.
0 = Desperate!

Now use the same scoring system to assess the power of other important people or groups of people in your organization. We have suggested your boss, your staff, your colleagues, etc., but you can easily customize this matrix for your own purposes. For example, if you were thinking about your chances of leading a particular project then you might assess your power against that of the other candidates; if you were thinking about the general influence of your department compared with others then you would put in your department and all the others.

Step 3

Total the scores in each vertical column. (For the matrix as it stands above, without any added factors which you may have put in, the maximum possible total for each vertical column is $6 \times 5 = 30$.) Looking at the figures, ask yourself these questions:

• Is it obvious where the power lies?
• Are there some big disparities of power between people or groups?

- Am I making best use of my strengths?
- How can I build up my weak areas of power?

Now total the scores across the columns for each factor, and compare these with the possible totals in each direction. Ask yourself the following questions:

- Is there a particular source of power in play here?
- How do I stand on that type?
- Is there a particularly under-used source of power here which I can bring into play?

FOLLOW-UP

Power is something which many of us feel wary about. There are good reasons for this. We have all suffered from others abusing their power over us and we have all used our own power in an abusive way. This starts at home and school and carries on into the world of work. One way of dealing with fear is to try and face the source.

However, power is just as frequently used in a good way, to protect the weak, to influence the unwise, to achieve valued ends. Power is inherent in all situations and in all relationships. Without power we can do nothing. In order that it should not corrupt us we need to understand it, how it works, and how it works in us.

Analysing your situation, through activities like 'Powerlines', is a simple way of quelling fear and may help you to use power wisely through understanding better and perhaps by seeing one or two things that you, or others, could do to help.

If you found this useful, a good short account of organizations as political systems is Chapter 6 of Gareth Morgan's *Images of Organisation* (Sage, 1986). Charles Handy's *Understanding Organisations* (Penguin, 1993, 4th edn) is a classic text which provides a good starting point for understanding cultural factors and how balances may shift.

Simon Baddeley and Kim James' article 'Owl, fox, donkey or sheep: political skills for managers', *Management Education and Development*, Vol. 18, Pt. 1, 1987, pp. 3–19 provides a useful model for managers who see political skills as an increasingly important element in their lives.

Activity 8

Differences and discrimination

LEARNING AREAS: SENSITIVITY TO EVENTS: Professional knowledge: Situational facts

The six jobs or achievements listed below on the left are those of six people listed on the right — but they have been jumbled up. Can you match them up correctly?

Job/Achievement	Person
A. Orchestral musician	1. 15-year-old with cerebral palsy
B. Embroidery designer	2. Woman with serious physical disability whose height is 3'11"
C. Steeplejack	3. Profoundly deaf person
D. Fighter Pilot	4. 55-year-old housewife
E. Front office receptionist for catering/tourism training organization	5. Person with two artificial legs
F. Winner of Whitbread literature prize	6. Colour-blind man

The true match is given at the end of this activity. However, the main purpose of this opening is to get you to reflect upon how you reacted to it. What went through your mind as you thought about the matching task?

Reflections of this kind can yield a lot of insight into how easily we use preconceived notions and stereotypes to discriminate amongst, and perhaps against, people. Stereotypes are the proverbial empty vessels, but people are discriminated against every day on grounds of gender, sexual orientation, social class, skin colour, age, disability, religion, etc. Taking human resources management seriously means making sure this does not happen in our organization.

For managers, at the most basic level, there are laws against sexual or racial discrimination, victimization and harassment—and, in Northern Ireland, against religious discrimination in employment. Employers with more than a certain number of staff have legal obligations to employ people with disabilities. With regard to anti-discriminatory laws it is essential to recognize that both *direct* and *indirect* discrimination are illegal.

Direct discrimination means treating a person or group less favourably on gender or racial grounds than others would be treated in similar circumstances. Indirect discrimination refers to unjustifiable requirements or conditions which, on the face of it, look equitable, but are not because a much smaller proportion of one gender or racial group can comply with them. An example would be restricting a management post to people aged 30–35—which could discriminate against women because more women of that age would be out of the labour market owing to parental responsibilities. (Additionally, of course, this example discriminates on the grounds of age against people who are older or younger. While this is not illegal, it is almost certainly not healthy in organizational terms.)

Nothing in the law prevents an employer from choosing the best person for a job, so long as there is no discrimination because of sex, marital status or race. This is an expanding area of law, and increasingly the subject of professional codes of practice and company policies. A good policy sets out how the organization will ensure that it achieves and maintains fairness and equal opportunity in all aspects of employment.

Recruitment and selection is an area that worries many managers because of the costs of getting it wrong. The activity below uses this situation to give you a framework for thinking about discriminatory or exclusionary practices.

The activity

The first step in a careful approach to recruitment and selection is creating a person specification (sometimes called a job specification) from a job description. This describes the qualities needed to do the job satisfactorily under (a) essential, (b) desirable; it can also be helpful to list (c) contra-indicators: things which genuinely disqualify someone for the work. A specification does not guarantee good selection, but it can greatly reduce errors. One of the best known formats for the person specification is the 'Seven Point Plan'.

Specifications can become biased in subtle ways—for instance, via fallacies, which may often be unconscious, about certain types of work being 'more suitable' for men or women. With senior jobs, factors of social class and status can become converted into standards of appearance, education or prestige social interests. 'Intelligence' is a heavily loaded concept, and so on.

The seven-point plan person specification

	Essential	Desirable	Contra-indicators
1. *Physical*—what does the work demand in terms of general health, physical strength or stamina, eyesight, hearing, speech, appearance?			
2. *Attainments*—education, training, experience, achievements			
3. *General intelligence*—specific indicators of reasoning ability and learning capacity			
4. *Special aptitudes*—e.g. mechanical, manipulative, mathematical, verbal/written expression, creativity			
5. *Interests*—e.g. intellectual, practical, active, social interests relevant to work			
6. *Disposition*—requirements in terms of working alone, getting on with others, using initiative, accepting responsibility, influencing, working under pressure			
7. *Circumstances*—e.g. travel from home, availability at certain times			

Table A8.1

Step 1

To see how much potential there is for a person specification to be influenced by factors other than those strictly necessary for the work, try the following exercise.

1. Thinking of most of the *managerial* jobs you know, how likely is recruitment and selection to discriminate, openly or indirectly, against some categories of people by:

- gender?
- marital status?
- age?
- skin colour?

- social class?
- disability?

Put your views in the form below. Work through all seven points and consider whether discrimination in recruitment and selection operates at managerial level with regard to gender, then marital status, and so on, working across the six factors given. If you think discrimination is likely to arise with regard to a factor, put an 'X' in the box. Otherwise leave it blank or put in a question mark.

Possible discriminatory factors

	Gender	Marital status	Age	Skin colour	Social class	Disability
1. Physical						
2. Attainments						
3. General intelligence						
4. Special aptitudes						
5. Interests						
6. Disposition						
7. Circumstances						

Table A8.2

Step 2

For each area of discrimination you have identified:

Who is likely to be discriminated against?

How is it likely to arise?

How can it be avoided?

Step 3

> In relation to your current sphere of influence, do you think discrimination affects any aspect of employment? If so, what needs to be done to eliminate it?

FOLLOW-UP

> This aspect of relationships at work may lead to difficult personal or organizational questions. In facing them, perhaps you can draw inspiration from Walter Winchell's dictum that 'Success is the reward of anyone who goes looking for trouble'.

> However, this issue is bigger than just about avoiding discrimination—important though that is. In the adaptive, learning organization we aim to make the most of all the people and their learning. A company which is discriminatory is also likely to be ineffective in terms of making the most of its resourceful humans.

> Sources of useful reading and information here include:

> *Job Analysis: A Practical Guide for Managers* by Michael Pearn and Rajvinder Kandola (Institute of Personnel Management, 1988) focuses mainly on job descriptions, while *Personnel Management: A New Approach* by Derek Torrington and Laura Hall (Prentice-Hall, 2nd edn, 1991) is more comprehensive in covering aspects of equal opportunity, as is William Werther and Keith Davis' *Human Resources and Personnel Management* (McGraw-Hill, 4th edn, 1993).

> *Pride against Prejudice: Transforming Attitudes to Disability* by Jenny Morris (Women's Press, 1991) is a powerful book; Deborah Clarke's *Women at Work* (Element, 1992) looks at factors which help or hinder women's advancement; *'Race' in Britain Today* by Richard Skellington and Paulette Morris (Sage Publications/Open University Press, 1992) is a good introduction to the issues for black people and the wider society.

Useful contacts

> (i) Royal Society for Disability and Rehabilitation (RADAR), 25 Mortimer St., London W1N 8AB Tel. 071 637 5400
> (ii) Royal National Institute for the Blind (RNIB) which has an employment network and three regional offices, 224 Great Portland St., London W1N 6AA Tel. 071 388 1266
> (iii) Equal Opportunities Commission (EOC) which has a free advisory service on sex discrimination matters regarding employment, education and training and a very useful list of

publications, Overseas House, Quay St., Manchester M3 3HN Tel. 061 833 9244

(iv) The Commission for Racial Equality (CRE) has a lot of useful publications concerning equal opportunities in employment, Elliot House, 10–12 Allington St., London SW1E 5EH Tel. 071 828 7022

(v) The Institute of Personnel Management (IPM) is another useful source of information about equal opportunities policy and practice, IPM House, Camp Rd., Wimbledon, London SW19 4UX Tel. 081 946 8100

Answers to matching task

A = 3 (Evelyn Glennie)
B = 6*
C = 4*
D = 5 (Sir Douglas Bader)
E = 2*
F = 1 (Christy Nolan, *Damburst of Dreams*)

* private individuals known to authors

Activity 9
Micro-political mapping

LEARNING AREAS: SENSITIVITY TO EVENTS: Social skills: Proactivity

One of the abilities which managers are increasingly expected to possess is that of political sensitivity or awareness. We have lots of words to describe this ability—we call it *nous* or being *street-wise, clued-up, on the ball*—and recognize it in people who somehow know who to talk to, who to agree with, who to disagree with, which meetings are the important ones to go to and so on. Equally we recognize the innocents among us who seem to have very little idea of what is going on around them. These people may be very knowledgeable or skilled in their own fields, but when it comes to how the organization works—of how things get done—they don't have a clue. Sometimes innocents are promoted to managerial positions where they can seriously constrain the efforts of their staff.

Among the knowing, however, are some who act with integrity and some who play games. Many managers enjoy some of the game-playing aspects of their jobs as part of the fun of being in the organization. But those for whom the game becomes the main issue we might call clever, but never wise. While innocents can exhibit a kind of wisdom, we would only use the word wise of someone who (a) knows what is going on, and (b) bases their actions on the longer term perspective based on personal values rather than short-term political advantage.

This activity cannot guarantee you wisdom, but it might help you to become a little more street-wise around your organization.

The activity

Step 1

First, think of a change which you want to make. It can be a small or a large one. Even small ones—such as changes in paperwork systems, furniture layout, meal times and so on—will illustrate the effects of power and politics very nicely. However, make sure it is a change which is important to you and which you intend to make.

Step 2

(i) Using the *Who's who?* worksheet below, list in the left-hand column all the people and groups who are involved in making the change or who will be affected by it.

(ii) Now list your views of the *interests* of each of these people or groups in the centre column. In thinking of interests it is useful to consider:

● *vested* interests—salary, resources, career prospects, territory, advantages, perks, etc.
● *ideological* interests—political or philosophical commitments
● *self*-interests—personal values, sense of personal and professional identity

Micro-political mapping: Who's who?

People/Group	Interests	Power sources

Table A9.1

(iii) Finally put down what you see as each person or group's main sources of power in the right-hand column. One classification of power sources is:

1. Position
2. Resources and rewards
3. Knowledge and expertise
4. Personal influence
5. Networks and gossip
6. Energy and stamina

You can find explanations of these in Activity 7, Powerlines.

Having listed all the people and groups involved and their interests and sources of power, to which of these do you need to pay special attention? If you have a long list, you may be feeling that it would be better to let sleeping dogs lie. This is one of the problems with analysing situations—it can lead to paralysis. However, that is not our intention here, we're hoping to empower you to act with political awareness and integrity!

The next step will help you to move on.

Step 3

Now consider the *orientation* of each of your people or groups to the change which you have in mind. The second worksheet below has two dimensions:

(i) Support/resist—is the person or group supportive of or resistant to the change?
(ii) Power—does the person or group have high or low power in this situation?

This gives four obvious locations:

Powerful and supportive	Powerful and resistant
Weak and supportive	Weak and resistant

Now mark your people or groups on the worksheet. You can either assign them simply to one of the quadrants or you can grade them carefully with regard to the vertical and horizontal scales.

Micro-political mapping : Change orientation

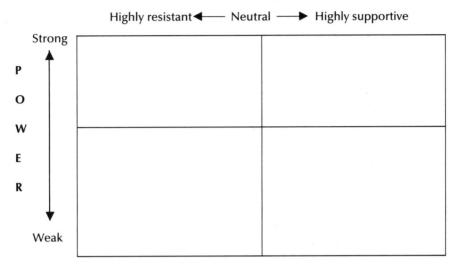

SUPPORT/RESIST

Highly resistant ◄─── Neutral ───► Highly supportive

Step 4

What does your picture look like? Does it show a critical mass of support for your change or does it show solid ranks of resistance?

In the latter case, should you rethink your ideas or reconsider your plans?

If, as often, the picture is more evenly balanced, what could you do to move it more towards supporting your change? Can you approach individuals or groups, for example, to:

- find out why resisters are resisting? Do they understand fully the change which is being proposed? What are their objections? Is there anything they would like which would change their orientation?
- ask powerful supporters to approach powerful resisters to try to 'get them on board' or at least to reduce their resistance?
- help those who are supportive but weak become more powerful? Perhaps the individuals or groups in this quadrant can be brought together to reduce isolation and to develop a mission and a sense of joint identity? Can they be encouraged to speak at meetings? Can their status be raised in any way?

FOLLOW-UP

Some people find it hard to understand why such thinking is useful in preparing to make changes. Nicolo Machiavelli is often invoked with his ruminations on 'whether it is better to be loved than to be feared' and his exhortations to 'be like a lion and a fox' (presumably, to be able to be forthright and honest as well as sly and devious). Some organizations do bear a passing resemblance to the Medici court, and if you happen to work in one of these then perhaps 'The Prince' is still as good a guide as any.

However, most organizations employ manners and methods which have moved on a bit over the last 500 years. Many, especially those which employ several professional or skill-based groups, are complicated to lead and to manage because all changes to the existing order tend to require a process of continuous negotiation. 'Micro-political mapping' will help you to become that bit more knowing and it should make your change efforts that bit more successful.

'Micro-political mapping' is taken from Kath Aspinwall *et al.*'s *Managing Evaluation in Education* (Routledge, 1992) which, despite the title, will be helpful to anyone thinking about change in complex organizations. Evaluation is the most political of activities, and the book contains lots of helpful ideas and activities. Chapter 5 of Gareth Morgan's *Images of Organisation* (Sage, 1986) is the best short account of organizations as political systems, and Simon Baddeley and Kim James' article 'Owl, fox, donkey or sheep: political skills for managers', *Management Education and Development*, Vol. 18, Pt. 1, 1987, pp. 3–19 provides another useful model of political skills for managers.

Activity 10
Credulous listening

LEARNING AREAS: SENSITIVITY TO EVENTS: Social skills: Balanced learning
habits

> If you want to know something about a person, ask—they just
> might tell you—George Kelly

George Kelly published his ideas almost 40 years ago, and the
implications are still emerging. Kelly believed that although the
world was real and not a figment of our imaginations, each person is
always individually trying to grasp and make sense of this world and
only ever partly succeeding. We all construct our own understandings and there are an infinite variety of alternative perceptions and
theories which we can make. He called these theories *personal
constructs* because they are the individual's unique ways of understanding his or her world. We do have common understandings
with others, but we only communicate well with them if we have a
sense of their value systems as well as our own.

Helen Jones, who works with Kelly's ideas, places great importance
on *credulous listening*, which implies:

 (i) believing that what the other person says is true for them; and
(ii) suspending our own ideas and constructs in order to understand the *personal constructs* of the other person.

Many of us find this very difficult. When we talk with others we
often internally translate what they are saying so that it matches our
own ideas. Sometimes our ideas, prejudices and assumptions get in
the way so much that we think 'Why is she telling me this?' or 'Here
he goes again blowing his own trumpet!', so that we can hardly hear
what they say at all.

In order to deal with this problem it can be helpful to try to
become—at least for a time—a *credulous listener*.

99

The activity

Step 1

(i) Choose a time when you know that you're going to have a meeting with someone whose ideas, values or beliefs you find difficult.

Decide that you will listen credulously to everything that they are going to say—yes, everything!

This means that you will be accepting that what they say is *true for them*.

(ii) Because credulous listening is difficult, set yourself a target, say, to listen credulously for 20 or 30 minutes. If possible, take a break at this point in order to jot down their ideas and perhaps to reflect them back to the person. Take the chance to check out whether you have fully understood the meanings and implications which the words have for the other person.

In order to listen credulously to the other person you also have to listen to yourself in order to suspend your own views. When you 'hear' yourself becoming incredulous, say to yourself 'What this person is saying is true for them, I don't have to agree or disagree, but just listen and try to understand what they are saying', or something similar—you get the idea.

If you have ever had to do any interviewing or counselling you may have had a taste of this experience, when your task is to enable the person to tell you *their* point of view, *their* taste, *their* perceptions. Even in this formal situation it can be very hard not to impose your own construction of events by tone of voice, raised eyebrows, etc., on what the other person is saying.

(iii) How did you do?

Did you really listen credulously?

Do you understand that person's view of the world better?

If you can answer 'Yes' to these questions, give yourself a pat on the back. As well as giving the other person that all too rare experience of being really listened to, you might well have learned something new for yourself. Through credulous listening we escape the limits of our own thoughts and imaginations and gain access to a wider world.

FOLLOW-UP

Practising credulous listening will give you one of the most valuable skills you are likely to find in this book. There is a variation which you can do on your own which we might call *credulous reading*. This reflects two other processes—loosening and tightening—which Kelly saw as central to his notion of people as experimenters continually testing their understanding of the world. Loosening (exploring and trying out ideas) and tightening (choosing options and making things happen) are continuous and reciprocal processes which help us to learn.

Next time you're reading a book, think about the *way* you're reading. Here are two possible extreme positions:

'Being taken over' by the story, being enamoured, getting lost in it (loosening)	'Reading for a purpose' ransacking the text for a specific end; instrumental; judgemental (tightening)

Depending on *how* you read it, you will take different things from the book. Of course, it's the same with people.

A good introduction to the ideas of George Kelly, whose book *The Psychology of Personal Constructs* (Norton, 1955) can be rather heavy going, is Peggy Dalton and Gavin Dunnett's *A Psychology for Living: Personal Construct Theory for Professionals and Clients* (Wiley, 1992). As the title suggests, this is a practical and applied text written in a straightforward and friendly way. Don Bannister and Fay Fransella's *Inquiring Man* (Croom Helm, 3rd edn, 1986) is a more formal but readable book which illustrates the uses of personal construct psychology and repertory grids.

Activity 11
Decision making

An important aspect of the manager's job concerns the making of decisions. Robert Townsend[1] commented that something like 40 per cent of the decisions he made while Managing Director of Avis turned out to be wrong in some way. Most important, though, he made them. It looks as though first-class managers average 50–60 per cent correct decisions. (It takes a first-class manager to admit this.) Most of us have a remarkable facility for justifying our actions or for 'rationalizing'. We do this even when not called to account by others; we justify ourselves to ourselves. If we did less of this we would recognize how many of our decisions turned out to be wrong, sometimes initial decisions which created a dozen crisis/ decision points. A manager's decision to authorize a new project will spawn dozens more as it gets under way—intermediate outcomes calling for intermediate decisions and so on.

All decisions are hedged about with uncertainty—otherwise there would be no decision to make—some being more uncertain than others.

Broadly speaking there are two ways of making decisions:

Following a 'rational' process of planning: specifying alternatives, criteria, and payoff probabilities until the 'correct' solution emerges.
Following 'hunches' or intuition: taking action without planning because action creates information and information reduces uncertainty.

Depending on training and personality most of us use one of these modes more than the other—even to the exclusion of the other. This is perhaps natural, but it limits our capacity for meeting different kinds of decisions. Complex decisions may demand the use of both modes at different times.

Activity

Below are some sample decisions. Although some may be complex we'll treat them as simple and say that one mode of decision making is more suitable than the other.

Step 1

Read each sample decision and decide whether it is 'rational' (Type A) or 'intuitive' (Type B).

1. Getting yourself from your place of work to a meeting in another specific location.
2. Being dropped anywhere in the country, without knowing where, with £1, and the task of getting home. Imagine yourself standing in open country surrounded by a light fog.
3. Choosing the means of communicating some minor redundancies in the company, given a 48-hour deadline and a partly unionized labour force.
4. Selecting a bonus payment scheme for a work section where workloads are extremely variable and where payment has previously been on a flat hourly rate.
5. Deciding how to approach your boss about a favour you want and knowing that he or she can be very moody and changeable.
6. Deciding how to run a particular appraisal interview.

You might well say that you would use both decision types as appropriate. We say that in *broad terms* the decisions split as shown in Table A11.1.

Decision	Type
1	A
2	B
3	A
4	A
5	B
6	B

Table A11.1   A = rational; B = intuitive.

Step 2

The choice of decision type has a very marked effect on how you behave when faced with a particular problem. Try thinking aloud about a couple of the decisions in the list above.

Jot down on a piece of paper the steps you would take to make the decisions set out as 1 and 2.

Then answer the following:

(a) Are your notes very similar for decisions 1 and 2, or very different?
(b) Which did you find easier: 1 or 2?

You probably found decision 1 easier to tackle.

Decision 1 is 'rational'; the goal is clear and there are relatively well-structured alternatives. In the jargon—there is a specific goal with limited goal paths. Therefore, a rational decision is possible by sifting the alternatives against the criteria and choosing appropriately. We can spell out this rational process using decision 1 as an example (Table A11.2).

Problem-solving stages	Decision 1
1. Analyse the problem in terms of: (a) How things are. (b) How I want things to be.	1. I am at work and I want to get to the meeting in London.
2. Specify *your objective* in terms of the change you want to bring about, i.e., A→B.	2. (Already stated in 1 above.)
3. Specify the alternative courses of action open to you to achieve the objective.	3. Go by: —car —train —taxi —bus —aeroplane —get a lift from a colleague
4. Specify the *criteria*, i.e., what characteristics must a course of action have to achieve your objective.	—I need to be there by 10 a.m. and I don't want to stay overnight (before or after). —It must not cost more than £20. —It would be useful to be able to read the papers for the meeting on the journey. —I need to be fresh on arrival.
5. Choose the alternative which best meets the criteria.	5. The train meets the criteria. The car fails on criteria three and four; the taxi on criterion two; the bus is noisy and fails on four; there is no plane until 10 a.m. and this fails on criterion one; travelling with a colleague is possible but would hinder criterion three.
6. Implement the alternative.	6. Catch the train.
7. Check whether you have achieved your goal, and if not, return to 1.	7. Did you get to the meeting on time and fresh?

Table A11.2

Decision 2 does not lend itself to such an analysis. There is a clear goal: you want to get home; but you have no idea where you are and there are no clearly structured alternative actions open to you. There is much more uncertainty in this situation than in decision 1. With this lack of information there is a limit to the amount of planning you can do before taking action. In well-structured situations *planning* can usefully precede *action*. In unstructured situations, where uncertainty predominates, it is better to get into action quickly because *action generates information*. In decision 2, an intelligent action is to walk in a fixed direction (not in a circle) because this would give you maximum chance of uncovering information: a stream; a path; a road; a clearing in the mist, etc. If you find a path then you clearly have a much more structured choice— whether to follow it and, if so, in which direction. As paths always lead from one place to another, you will tend to follow it in the hope of finding out where you are, i.e., to generate more information. Eventually, you will generate enough information to know what kind of a problem you have in getting home, and what the alternatives are. You are then back in a decision 1-type 'rational' process.

In conditions of uncertainty, *action has to precede planning*, because action generates the information required for planning. Or to put it another way, the first objective in uncertain situations is to generate information. You choose an action to this end and pursue it until further information is obtained, at which point planning may be appropriate.

In decision 5 there are no obvious alternative courses of action because the boss is *unpredictable*. A carefully planned strategy could be disastrous—a plan possesses a momentum which is hard to modify. The best approach would be to keep on neutral ground until his or her behaviour provides a clue to his or her mood, after which you can plan what action to take.

Decision 6 is a similar situation unless you regard it as a one-way process—in which case you can adopt a 'rational' approach without the need to generate information about the other person's feelings and views. Most interpersonal situations demand the *action before planning* approach. This is the area of decision making which creates many problems for managers. Those who are able to suspend their planning skills to generate sufficient information about alternatives and criteria *according to other people* will usually make better decisions. They are more 'socially skilled' than managers who impose a previously-planned 'rational' decision upon others.

To summarize: use the 'rational' process for well-structured situations; use an *action before planning* approach to situations where there is little or no information (you have first to be able to admit/ recognize that there is little or no information).

The following advice is useful in uncertain situations:

- Regard obtaining information as an objective in itself.
- Be prepared to get quickly into action of a kind which will generate information.
- Be prepared to go through many cycles of action → information → planning → action.

All this can be fitted into the 'rational' decision-making process if you recognize its cyclical nature; the need to start with information-getting as the objective; the need to move into action on an experimental basis.

Step 3

If you think you understand the difference between the two approaches to decision making, this step will test you further.
Reflect upon a recent or current decision and ask yourself:

- Has 'information-getting' been an objective?
- Has there been enough experimental action?
- Have I picked up all the information available from experimental action and from elsewhere?
- Have I analysed the available information carefully and did it result in improved understanding?

FOLLOW-UP

There are a number of well-known courses and books on decision making and problem solving. *Strategic Decision-making* by Chris Gore, Kate Murray and Bill Richardson (Cassell, 1992) contains clear models and realistic cases and is good on developing decision-making processes. John Harvey-Jones' *Managing to Survive* (Heinemann, 1993) is about deciding to change and enjoying it, while Peter Drucker's *Managing the Non-profit Organisation* is full of sense and deep knowledge.

Finally, in the IT era you might want to consider some of the software packages. Spreadsheet programs allow for easy 'what if' or sensitivity projections and forecasts, while project planning packages enable you to plan your own critical paths. *Mastering Spreadsheets and Forecasts* by Malcolm Secrett (Pitman, 1993) is a simple, step-by-step guide to computerized budgeting.

REFERENCES

1. Townsend, R., *Up the Organization*, Coronet Books, 1971.

Activity 12
Planning and decision-making techniques

LEARNING AREAS: ANALYTICAL SKILLS: Professional knowledge

Numerous planning and decision-making techniques, each with many variations, are available to managers. Opinions vary about the usefulness of such techniques, a common criticism being that techniques work well on classroom type problems specially designed to show how they work, but that problems that managers actually experience rarely fit neatly with the techniques.

However, there are a number of basic techniques (with variations) which any manager could usefully know about. From the point of view of self-development in the area of decision-making and planning techniques, there are plenty of resources available, with books, manuals, and courses on all of them. Most large organizations will have specialists from whom advice could be sought.

Here we provide you with an exercise to check and extend your awareness of some current techniques. If any of them seem pertinent to your problem and worth going into further, you should look for further reading, courses, or help from experts.

There are two points to make about management techniques which stem from the fact that various individuals have *specialized* in each of the techniques and devoted much work to them. They have developed variations and refinements of each of the basic techniques, and entered into complex debate with each other about various points of application. They have, understandably, been most interested in complex and ambitious applications of these techniques, often involving project teams working on a single problem over many months, sometimes making extensive use of computers. Against this background we make two claims that you might like to consider (particular experts might disagree with us!):

1. The *core idea* in each technique is relatively simple (as are most good ideas) and easily grasped by a normal, intelligent person.

2. Application of the techniques can be brief. A simple useful application of most of the techniques can be carried out in 15 minutes on the back of an envelope. Indeed, once the idea of each technique has been grasped, it should be possible to incorporate some of the key ideas and principles into your thinking, and thus apply the techniques 'inside your head'. The main payoff from studying management techniques may be from the general effect this has on how you think, rather than through formal and explicit application of the techniques.

Activity

Step 1

Look at the list of techniques/methods below, and ask yourself if they mean anything to you. Write under each what you know about them.

Critical path analysis/network planning.

Value analysis.

Linear programming.

Break-even-point analysis.

Cost-benefit analysis.

Cost-effectiveness analysis.

Discounted cash flow.

Step 2

Compare your understanding with the brief descriptions below:

Critical path analysis/network planning. A method of planning for complex, often one-off, projects like putting up a building, installing a new plant, moving an operation from one location to another. In such operations a whole series of tasks have to be done in the right order at the right time for an overall objective to be achieved on time.

The overall method is to list the tasks to be done, work out the order of priorities draw a 'map' of operations something like Fig. A12.1 (though, of course, much more complicated). The idea is that to do the overall job one has to work down all the 'paths' from left to right. From here it is possible to plan time and resources for each task, and work out which sequence of operations, if delayed, would delay the whole project (this sequence is the 'critical path').

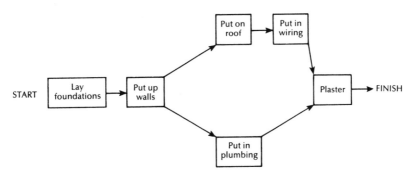

Figure A12.1

Value analysis. This is a process of taking something that is produced, at a cost, to perform a function (usually a product, but it can be a service) and analysing what the cost goes on (parts, assembly tasks, etc.), assessing what these cost elements actually contribute to the performance of the product's function. On the basis of this, ways of reducing the cost of the product without impairing its ability to perform its function can be sought.

Linear programming. The linear programming problem is exemplified by the farmer who has available a choice of feedstuff for the cattle, each at different prices, each with different proportions of, say, protein, fat, and carbohydrate in it. The farmer knows what the cattle require, in terms of minimum quantities of the three forms of food. The problem is to work out the cheapest combination of the available foodstuffs to meet these requirements.

Break-even-point analysis. What it costs to make most mass-produced goods can be split more or less into 'fixed' and 'variable' costs. Fixed costs are those which are incurred once you have decided to set up facilities for production. Variable costs are those that increase in proportion to the number of items you make. In car manufacture, setting up a production line is a fixed cost, the materials and labour that go into making the cars is a variable cost, because for each extra car you produce the more you need of them. The cost of producing various numbers of products can therefore be shown on a graph like that of Fig. A12.2.

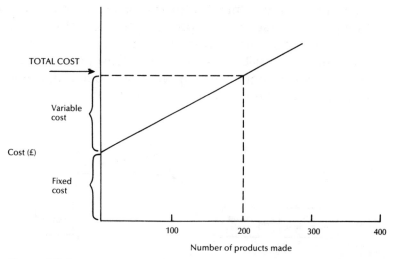

Figure A12.2

Another graph can be drawn (Fig. A12.3) relating revenue to number of products sold.

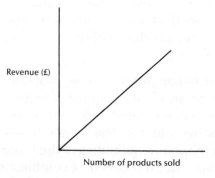

Figure A12.3

The slope of the line is determined by the price. The two graphs can be put on top of each other (Fig. A12.4).

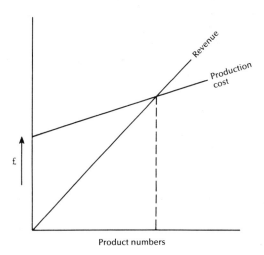

Figure A12.4

The break-even point is where the two lines meet. At this point revenue from sales = production cost and you have 'broken-even'. Make and sell more than that and you have a financial return. Make and sell less and you are making a loss.

This kind of analysis is particularly relevant to pricing decisions, and deciding whether it is worth going into a certain line of business.

Cost-benefit analysis. This is simply looking at decision 5 in terms of what it would *cost* to go for each alternative, and what the benefit would be from pursuing each alternative, in cost terms. Thus, for example, a transport firm might evaluate different makes and sizes of lorries for its fleet in terms of purchase cost, maintenance costs, and running costs against the return it would get over the lorries' lives.

Cost-effectiveness analysis. Cost-effectiveness analysis is intended for situations where it is difficult to quantify the benefit side of the equation. It starts from the point of assuming that one wants to do something, looks for alternatives that are equally effective in doing it, and chooses the cheapest. Thus, for example, a firm may decide that it must provide its employees with a canteen affording a given level of service at given hours, and at a given meal price. It then looks at alternative ways of doing this, for example hiring a catering contractor or taking on staff, works out what the alternatives cost, and makes a choice.

Discounted cash flow. Many business decisions involve choosing a line of action that entails making expenditures at different points of time in the future, in the hope of generating revenue at other points of time in the future. Thus, in going into the transport business there is the initial cost of vehicles, and the further costs of maintenance, fuel, and drivers' wages spread over the life of the vehicles, plus expenditure on replacing mechanical parts, etc. coming in should be a steady flow of revenue from freight charges paid by customers. A decision like this involves working out if one would end up better off by going in for this enterprise, and better off by enough to make it worth the trouble.

Because £100 now is not worth the same as the promise of £100 in one year's time, it is not enough to calculate expected cash flow out (costs) and in (revenue). Discounted cash flow is allowing for this by correcting expected costs and revenues at different times to their value at the same time (usually now). This is done by assuming a discount rate (which might be the interest rate at which money can be borrowed, or an estimate of inflation, or a rate fixed by the organization for the purpose) and using this to 'correct' the value of revenues and costs.

If the rate of 20 per cent is assumed (as an estimate of likely inflation, or because this is the cost of borrowing money to finance the project), the £100 would be worth £120 in one year's time, and therefore £100 in one year's time is worth

$$\pounds \frac{100 \times 100}{120} = \pounds 83\tfrac{1}{3} \text{ now.}$$

Cost or revenue of £100 in one year's time would be counted as £83⅓ now. Thus all costs and revenues of the project can be corrected to current value equivalents to get a more accurate estimate of the value of the project.

FOLLOW-UP

1. Think carefully whether any of these techniques 'fit' any of your problems.
2. 'Do it yourself' on a specific problem, working out the way from the descriptions above.
3. Choose the techniques that interest you and follow them up with further reading and study.

If you want to improve your financial know-how, Roger Oldcorn's *Accounting for Managers* (Routledge, 1993) is a 100-page introduction for non-financial managers, while *Business Finance for Decision-makers* by E. J. McLaney (Pitman, 1991) has learning exercises and assignments to apply to your own workplace and even includes some right answers!

The big classic on marketing is Philip Kotler's *Marketing Management: Analysis, Planning, Implementation and Control* (Prentice-Hall, 7th edn, 1991). He also has an interesting volume of cases, *Strategic Marketing for Non-profit Organisations* (Prentice-Hall, 4th edn, 1991).

Activity 13
Choosing solutions with a chance

LEARNING AREAS: ANALYTICAL SKILLS: Proactivity: Social skills

One of the criticisms levelled at 'rational problem solving' is that it is easier to decide what needs to be done than to make it happen—to implement the decision. The logical thing is to take 'implementability' into account when choosing solutions; you must be able to put them into practice.

Here are three checklists of 'implementability' criteria, taken from consultants' folklore (consultants have big implementation problems since they rarely have access to formal authority to enforce solutions):

(From Alec Roger):
For a solution to be acceptable it must be seen as:

- technically feasible (it must look as though it will actually work);
- politically acceptable (will not involve changes seen as against the interests of anyone powerful enough to stop it);
- administratively convenient (consistent with the customs, procedures and practices of the organization, so that it is feasible for the people who actually have to do the work).

(From Tom Lupton):
For a solution to be worth attempting there needs to be conviction by all concerned:

- that it will work (technically feasible as above);
- that 'they' will work it ('they' is everybody whose cooperation is needed to put it into practice);
- that it will pay (in money or whatever terms are seen as important).

(From Don Binsted):
For a recommended course of action to be accepted:

- it must be seen as relevant to some problem that really is bothering the people who have to accept or reject it;
- it must suggest clearly a state of affairs that would be generally accepted as better;
- it must offer at least a first and useful step towards a better state of affairs, which is easy for the people concerned to take.

Activity

Choose a problem you are having in getting something done, or in getting an idea, solution, or proposal accepted.

Now draw up a list, as in Table A13.1, of the people involved, concerned, or affected by your idea. Write their names in the left-hand column. These are the people to whom you must 'sell' your proposal.

In the middle column, note the 'implementability' criteria that each of these people will require if they are to accept your proposal. As a guideline you can use the sets of criteria given above, but you will probably be able to identify other criteria specific to particular individuals or groups.

Other parties concerned	Criteria by which other parties will be judging the idea	Match/Mismatch between criteria and proposal

Table A13.1

If you cannot identify appropriate criteria in some cases—discuss it with the people involved. It is also a good idea, when you think you know the criteria that the various people are looking for, to check out your perception with them. It is surprising how often we make false assumptions about other people—their needs, motives, and interests.

Having identified and checked the criteria that involved/affected parties will use to judge your suggestion, use the final column to note the way in which your idea meets, or fails to meet, each criterion.

When you have done this, you will have a much clearer idea of the likelihood of your plan gaining acceptance, and you will have identified changes you may need to make to have a better chance of acceptance.

FOLLOW-UP

This activity should be incorporated into your on-going managerial life. By being sensitive to the interests of other people, and bearing these in mind when proposing changes, you will have a much greater chance of getting changes accepted and of being an effective member of a management team.

How to Influence Others at Work by Dick McCann (Heinemann, 1988) contains models and ideas for breaking deadlocks and coming to workable solutions. Chapters 7 and 8 are particularly relevant and there is a useful introduction to neuro-linguistic programming (NLP), a theory and practice of interpersonal communication.

Activity 14
Role set analysis

The concept of 'role' has come to have a central place in management theories. Decision-making roles, leadership roles, supervisory roles are a few examples of the frequent use we make of this term.

The term 'role' is borrowed from the stage where an actor may perform in the role of soldier, king, or lover. In this sense, it is an act or a series of actions. In life we perform many roles—as wife/husband; father/mother; neighbour; daughter/son. Although we remain ourselves—as does the actor passing from role to role—our behaviour is largely determined by the role we are occupying at a given time. Indeed, if we don't alter behaviour to fit into the appropriate role we run into trouble—as you will if you speak to your spouse on the phone at work as you might to a junior working colleague. Errors of this sort—which we sometimes make—are the results of 'role' conflict.

Role conflict occurs because all roles make demands on our behaviour. Attached to each role are the other people—'significant others'—who make up the role network. These people all have expectations about the way in which the person occupying the role should behave. For example, as a manager, my boss expects me to motivate and control my staff; my staff expect me to help them to provide them with the means to do their work; my fellow managers expect me to cooperate and liaise with them on jobs which affect us both.

Role conflict occurs in a number of ways:

- Because two people make opposing or conflicting demands on the role-holder, e.g., the boss who wants the manager to discipline his staff who, in turn, want protection from the boss.
- Because we fill many different roles in quick succession and the demands of one role may conflict with the demands of another,

e.g., my role as a manager conflicts with my roles as partner and parent when I need to work late or at the weekend.

- Because roles carry expectations for behaviour which we personally do not find congenial, e.g., in my role as a manager I have to overlook certain commercial practices, such as giving 'gifts' to clients, which I disapprove of from an ethical viewpoint.

Role conflict is one of the major causes of managerial stress—to avoid stress, role relationships have to be managed like any other part of the job. Role is also an important concept because all our social behaviour is conducted in roles—our actual 'selves' or 'personalities' can never be directly observed.

The value of studying your role as a manager is that:

- You clarify your position within your organization.
- You establish what demands and expectations are made on you in your role.
- You identify possible and actual areas of conflict which helps to reduce the stress.
- You lay the foundations for improving your role performance and hence your general ability as a manager.

Activity

This activity is designed to achieve the four goals outlined above. All you need is a pen and some paper.

Step 1

Take a large sheet of paper and draw a circle in the middle to represent the role you occupy at work. Label this circle, e.g., 'Office Manager' (J. Brown). Now draw in around the periphery smaller circles to represent all the 'significant others' in the role network of the office manager. These are all the people who make demands upon and have expectations about the role. In addition, the role has reciprocal expectations and makes demands upon them.

You can show the strength of a particular link by making that 'significant other' nearer the centre. Those people with whom you have daily contact probably make more demands and have more expectations of you than those you meet weekly. The role network for the office manager might look like Fig. A14.1.

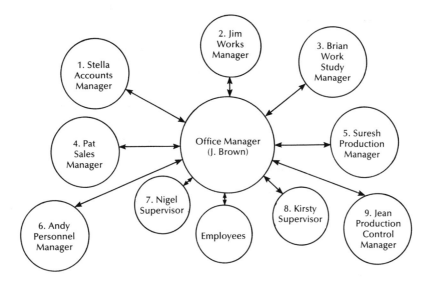

Figure A14.1

Step 2

When you have completed your role network it is a useful idea to ask someone else's views about it.

Have you included all significant role relationships?

How different is your role network from others around you?

How does it feel to be the 'person-in-the-middle' serving all these masters?

Step 3

If you are satisfied that you have included all the vital role relationships in your job, take another sheet of paper and make a chart. Put down on the left-hand side of the page all the roles which make demands upon your role. Put across the top three columns: 'Their demands/expectations of me'; 'My expectations and demands of them'; 'Possible conflict areas'.

The office manager's chart might look like Table A14.1.

Role	Their demands/ expectations of me	My expectations/ demands of them	Possible conflict areas
Supervisors (2)	1. Fair allocation of work	1. Achieve set work targets	
	2. Support for their actions	2. Deal with most grievances and people problems	Supervisor actions especially on discipline and grievances are not always consistent with company personnel policy
	3. Personal support e.g., to listen and be available		
	4. To provide resources to allow them to get the work done	3. Keep me informed about a variety of things, e.g., current workloads; supply of materials; personnel issues, etc.	
	5. Set realistic work targets	4. Be proactive— set own work targets in consultation with me	Supervisors dependent on me—will not take responsibility
Employees (16)	1. To treat them fairly	1. To work well and achieve work targets	
	2. To arbitrate over matters of disagreement with supervisors		Cannot satisfy both employees' demands on me to arbitrate *and* supervisors' demands for support of their actions
AND SO ON . . .			

Table A14.1

Step 4

There are a number of ways in which this role chart may help.

First, do you know what are all the demands and expectations of you? Are you sure you have them right? It is not unknown for managers confronted with this question to fail even where their boss is concerned.

Obviously if you don't know—check it out.

Second, does your perception of their expectations/demands of you fit with theirs? If you asked them would they agree with what you'd written?

The obvious way to check this is to ask them—if you can.

Last, what conflicts appear—between you and your role demands—between different expectations, etc.?

How can you resolve or cope with these?

Sometimes the answer is fairly simple. For example, on the office manager's role chart (Table A14.1), the first conflict area—'Supervisor actions especially on discipline and grievances are not always consistent with company personnel policy'—perhaps points to a training need.

FOLLOW-UP

Rosemary Stewart's *Managing Today and Tomorrow* (Macmillan, 1991) offers ways of thinking about the discretion you have in the managerial role and how this is affected by your role set. On the question of teams, Meredith Belbin's *Team Roles at Work* (Butterworth-Heinemann, 1993) extends his earlier ideas on understanding the interaction of roles and how you can get the best from a team.

Activity 15
Planning change

LEARNING AREAS: ANALYTICAL SKILLS: Proactivity

This activity consists of a planning tool designed to help you analyse events and problems from an action point of view. The tool is developed from a systems approach to problems and the basic idea is generally credited to Kurt Lewin whose 'field theory' described a field of forces or pressures acting on any particular event at any particular time.[1] All situations can be seen as being in temporary equilibrium, i.e., the forces acting to change the situation are balanced by the forces acting to resist the change.

We can depict this with a simple diagram (Fig. A15.1).

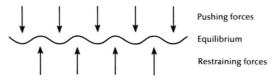

Pushing forces

Equilibrium

Restraining forces

Figure A15.1

Being able to accept this view of social situations may be something of a problem itself. This view of events is a dynamic one, which sees temporariness in all things and requires a somewhat existential standpoint. What it does offer to the manager is the opportunity of seeing situations as being potentially changeable—if he can identify the forces and seek to change their direction or strength.

Use this activity for a problem that has been worrying you and which seems intractable. The Force Field Analysis will make the options clearer and bring a vague problem into focus and be more 'do-able'.

Activity

This invites you to carry out a Force Field Analysis of a particular problem which is facing you at present. It proceeds in a number of stages which include a worked example with which to compare yours.

Step 1

Choose a problem and write it down.

It must be a real one which concerns you right now. The example taken here is that of a manager concerned about the rapid rise of accidents in his section.

Step 2

Define the problem in specific terms.

Who is involved?

What is the magnitude of the problem?

What other factors bear on the situation?

For example, accidents have risen in Department B over the last six months.

Days lost per month through accidents were averaging $5\frac{1}{2}$ per cent at that time; they have now risen to 10 per cent. Relevant factors may include a recent influx of new operatives and a change in bonus system to encourage greater output.

Step 3

Now state specifically how you would like to influence or change the situation. Try to make this as measurable as possible, so that you can set a clear target and know when you are reaching it. Sometimes this may not be possible, but try.

For example, 'I would like to reduce the days lost per month through accidents to, say, 5 or 6 per cent.'

Step 4

Looking at the problem as a temporary equilibrium held in place (for the moment) by pushing and restraining forces, list these forces operating on your problem.

(a) What are the forces which would move the present situation towards my goal? (PUSHING FORCES)

   (i)

   (ii)

(iii)

(iv)

(v)

(vi)

(b) What are the forces resisting or stopping the situation approaching my goal? (RESTRAINING FORCES)

(i)

(ii)

(iii)

(iv)

(v)

(vi)

For example, on the problem of reducing Department B's accident rate:

(a) PUSHING FORCES (to reduce accident rate):

(i) Manager's desire to lower the rate;
(ii) Company's concern at its image;
(iii) Employee's concern at injuries and costs incurred;
(iv) Union concern at injuries and costs incurred;
(v) Planned safety training courses for union representatives.

(b) RESTRAINING FORCES (tending to increase accident rate):

(i) Influx of new operators trained under government 'crash-course' scheme;
(ii) Company's need for increased output;
(iii) New individual bonus to increase output;
(iv) Casual attitude of younger employees concerning general behaviour and use of safety equipment;
(v) Resentment of some older employees at being pushed on output;
(vi) Attitude of older employees to safety regulations.

Make sure you have listed all the forces operating on the problem. Have you included:

- the motivations of individuals and groups involved?
- organizational policies and procedures?
- outside forces operating in the work environment?

Step 5

When all the forces are listed, rank them as being of

$$
\left.\begin{array}{l}
\text{HIGH} \\
\text{MEDIUM} \\
\text{LOW}
\end{array}\right\} \text{POWER}
$$

Do this for both PUSHING and RESTRAINING FORCES.

Step 6

Now diagram the forces using the length of the arrows to indicate the magnitude of the force. In the example in Fig. A15.2 the Manager's desire to reduce the rate is a HIGH power PUSHING force, while the casual attitude of younger employees is a MEDIUM power RESTRAINING force.

Step 7

Now prepare a strategy for changing the situation.

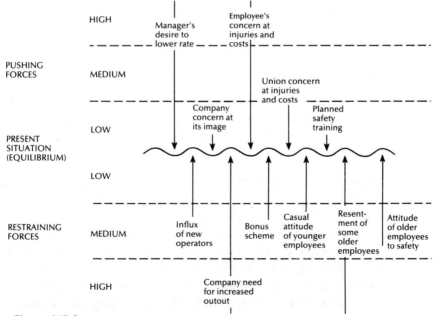

Figure A15.2

Remember:

(a) *That if you increase PUSHING forces you often create greater resistance in people and in systems.*
(b) *Change is most easily accepted when it requires a minimum of effort and disruption.*

Can you:

(a) Maintain PUSHING forces, but reduce any of the RESTRAINING forces?
(b) Find new PUSHING forces?
(c) If you must PUSH more, choose forces which do not increase resistance?
(d) Divert any RESTRAINING forces to new targets or in new directions?
(e) Are you sure that it is not one of your PUSHING forces which created the problem in the first place? Would a reduction in this PUSH also reduce the RESTRAINING force?

Your strategy should include the following steps:

(a) The stages to occur in sequence, with rough timings. Activity 12—'Planning and Decision-Making Techniques'—may help here.
(b) The resources you will need at each stage, particularly people who can help.
(c) Sub-goals to evaluate against in checking your progress. (A single far-off goal is somewhat daunting in its unattainability and difficult to plan against.)

FOLLOW-UP

As an analysis tool, Force Field Analysis can be used to examine any problem situation. More than just a technique, it is a way of seeing situations as being only in temporary equilibrium and amenable to change.

Change and how to implement it in organizations has attracted a huge literature in recent years. Roger Plant's *Managing Change and Making it Stick* (Fontana, 1987) is an excellent short guide to the nuts and bolts. Rosabeth Moss Kantor's work centres on this theme and she is usually good value. *When Giants Learn to Dance: Mastering the Challenge of Strategy, Management and Careers in the 1990s* (Simon & Schuster, 1989) is a clear-sighted blockbuster. Richard Beckhard and Wendy Pritchard's *Changing the Essence* (Jossey-Bass, 1992) is also worth a read. David Casey's *Managing Learning in*

Organisations (Open University Press, 1993), written for facilitators, is a fine little book concerned with working on learning with individuals, groups and teams.

REFERENCES

1. Lewin, K., *Field Theory in Social Science*, Harper, 1951.

Activity 16
Analysis of experiences

LEARNING AREAS: ANALYTICAL SKILLS: Balanced learning habits: Self-knowledge: Sensitivity to events

The successful manager is able to sense what is happening in work situations, being aware of the elements and factors involved, and of the way in which these factors are complexly related. When successful, we can recognize the effects of these factors on our own behaviour and, conversely, the effects of our behaviour on these factors. We are able to use this awareness and sensitivity to learn from everyday experiences.

One relatively long-term method of developing these abilities is through continued use of a 'Personal Journal' (Activity 6). However, there are times when a more detailed analysis is useful, and for these this particular activity can be recommended.

To save you checking back, we set out again here the same model of an individual's behaviour in a situation.

1. *The individual's FEELINGS:* the way we behave is very much determined by our feelings in a given situation. We are often unaware—or at best only partly aware—of the nature of our feelings and the effect they are having. In our society there is a tendency to suppress or deny feelings—'the stiff upper lip' is still much admired—but if you are to be in control of your behaviour, it is essential to be sensitive to your feelings and their effects.

2. *The individual's THOUGHTS AND IDEAS:* in any situation the individual lives through a number of thoughts and ideas. Important among these are the factors perceived in a situation and ideas about courses of action. These will depend on the various elements in the current situation and will be influenced by the individual's assumptions and the perceptions brought in from previous experiences. Also important will be the new thoughts and ideas triggered off by the new situation.

3. *The individual's ACTION-TENDENCIES:* The individual will have various action-tendencies: predispositions to certain types of action. For example, in committee and disagreeing strongly with the chairperson, we may nonetheless say nothing because we are scared of challenging authority. This fear or lack of self-confidence will result in an action-tendency of saying/doing nothing.

Another action-tendency could be described as precipitous: a strong need to *do* something rather than think things out carefully—a tendency which leads to over-hasty action.

Action-tendencies are internal motivations or forces that push individuals towards certain types of action or inaction.

These three elements each influence the individual's behaviour. Take the example of a manager in committee. The chairperson seems to be supporting something with which I, the manager, disagree. My thoughts/ideas are that what has been said are wrong. As a result my *feelings* are those of concern or excitement. However, due to my parallel feeling of fear of ridicule, or fear of challenging authority, my *action-tendency* is to say nothing.

My behaviour in this situation will depend upon which of the three elements wins out. Will my ideas and half my feelings overcome my action-tendency, leading to my making a soundly presented contribution? Or will my other feelings combine with my negative action-tendencies, leading me to remain silent? Or again, perhaps my feelings and action-tendencies will result in my making a fumbling, incoherent statement—i.e., preventing my beautifully logical ideas from getting a fair hearing.

The elements depend on each other. For example, my thoughts and ideas about what is being said may well depend upon my feelings about the person saying it—and vice versa. We can see that this model of behaviour, although simple, represents a very complicated situation. This can be shown as in Fig. A16.1, emphasizing the links between thoughts/ideas, feelings, and action-tendencies.

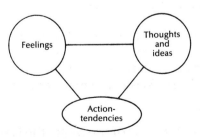

Figure A16.1

Feelings, thoughts/ideas, and action-tendencies don't exist in a vacuum. They arise in response to some situational stimulus (in itself affected by previous events). They result in behaviour, which leads to a new situation (Fig. A16.2).

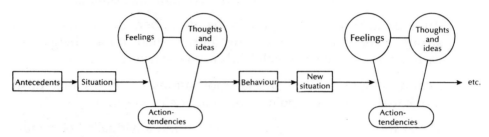

Figure A16.2

Activity

To develop skill in using this activity, you are recommended to approach it in two steps. The first looks at some past events and analyses them. When you have got used to doing this, you then move on to the second step and analyse current events—situations that are still on-going and not yet resolved.

Step 1

Choose a recent significant event or situation. 'Significant' means something challenging, worrying, or difficult. Choose a situation that you consider you handled well—or one which you regard as a failure.

Identify the individuals who, in addition to yourself, were involved.

Cast your mind back to the circumstances leading up to the event. Try to recall your feelings, thought/ideas, action-tendencies, and behaviour. Note these down, using Table A16.1 as a framework.

Now try to identify the feelings, thoughts/ideas, action-tendencies, and behaviour of each of the other persons who were significantly involved. This will be difficult; we can seldom say that we *know* how someone else is feeling. What we do is estimate or assume and you need to do that here.

If you have difficulty filling out this part of the table, the best source of information is the people themselves.

Check out with them how they were feeling, thinking, acting, behaving. You will always find it instructive to check the validity of your judgement by checking with the people involved.

At this stage think about the significance of the feelings that you were unable to identify, or that you assumed incorrectly.

Are you better at estimating feelings, or ideas, or action-tendencies?

Are there some people whose reactions you can perceive accurately, and others you cannot?

Now move on. Note down your perceptions of your own and others' responses *during* the event. Again, check with other people if necessary. Next note down the responses *after* the event.

People involved	Responses	Before the event	During the event	After the event
Me	My feelings			
	My thoughts/ideas			
	My action-tendencies			
	My actual behaviour			
Other 1	Their feelings			
	Their thoughts/ideas			
	Their action-tendencies			
	Their actual behaviour			
Other 2	Their feelings			
	Their thoughts/ideas			
	Their action-tendencies			
	Their actual behaviour			
etc.	etc.			

Table A16.1

Study your tabled notes and answer the following:

(a) In what ways were responses related to each other? What caused what?
(b) How do you feel about the way you handled the situation? What, if anything, could you have done differently? What do you think the consequences would have been?
(c) What do you learn from this?

Step 2

When you have practised this method of situational analysis over four or five past, significant events, apply it to a current situation — something of significance with which you are now involved.

(a) Analyse the situation so far. Check out your perceptions of other people's responses.
(b) So far, how are the various responses involved?
(c) How do you feel about the way the situation is shaping up so far? What are you going to do? What do you think the consequences will be?
(d) Do what you have decided to do.
(e) Continue with the analysis. Are the effects as predicted?
(f) Repeat steps (c)–(e) until you think the event is over.
(g) What have you learned from this event? What are the implications of this learning for your future actions?

FOLLOW-UP

This way of looking at situations should become part of your everyday managerial life. You should start considering situations in terms of the perceptions and responses of the other people involved — checking these out to make sure that you are not basing your actions on invalid assumptions.

Activity 17
Catastrophic contingencies

LEARNING AREAS: ANALYTICAL SKILLS: Creativity: Emotional resilience:
Proactivity: Self-knowledge

Many managers, faced with complex decisions, find themselves
blocked in by the fear of 'what if . . .?' Faced with uncertainty,
doubt, and the possibility of a bad, even catastrophic consequence
to our action, we tend towards stress and the inability to act.

This activity is designed to help you overcome this kind of blockage.

Step 1

Next time you are faced with a difficult problem, involving uncertainty, risk, or doubt—write down, first, the various courses of
action open to you. Then list the worst possible things that could
happen if everything went wrong. What are the worst catastrophes
that could occur?

Step 2

Take each catastrophe in turn and imagine that it really has happened. How do you feel in this disastrous situation? Is it so awful, or
were your fears exaggerated? Again, imagining that it has already
happened: What are you going to do now? From this catastrophic
situation what are your plans? How are you going to cope with it?
What could you have done to lessen its bad effects? (Imagine
yourself saying 'things wouldn't be so bad if only I . . .'.)

Step 3

When you have answered these questions you will probably find
that:

(a) Many possible catastrophes are not really as bad as your first,
unconsidered fears.

(b) You have identified some of the plans and actions that you can implement to lessen either the probability of the catastrophe's occurrence, or the severity of its effects.

(c) You have prepared some contingency plans for coping with the catastrophe should it occur. These will be helpful in themselves and, by reducing the ambiguity and helplessness of the situation, you will have lessened your fear of it.

You should now be able to overcome the blockage and make your decisions.

FOLLOW-UP

When drawing up your contingency plans Activities 34 ('Action Planning'), 15 ('Planning Change') and 13 ('Choosing Solutions with a Chance') will be helpful. Steven Schnaars' *Megamistakes: Forecasting and the Myth of Rapid Technological Change* (The Free Press, 1989) is entertainingly relevant, especially for over-confident forecasters.

Activity 18
Budgetary control*

LEARNING AREAS: ANALYTICAL SKILLS: Professional knowledge

Budgeting is the financial evaluation of an action plan prepared in advance. It is a planning and control technique used to improve business effectiveness and follows a sequential process:

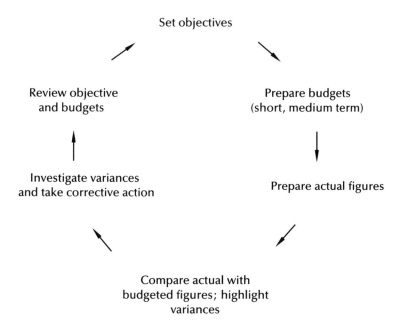

The first step in the process is to set objectives, e.g., to maximize profit; achieve a 25 per cent return on capital employed; increase market share by 30 per cent; survive; and so on.

Once the objectives are determined they are translated into a financial plan of action (the budget). Budgets are usually prepared

*This activity was designed by Graham Axelby, Senior Lecturer, Department of Accountancy and Professional Studies, Sheffield City Polytechnic.

in detail for the first 12 months and then in less detail for the next few years.

Since sales are often the limiting factor, the sales budget is prepared first, followed by the finished goods stock budget, raw materials budget, wages budget, etc., through to the debtors and creditors' budget. All of these are brought together in the master budget which is summarized in a profit and loss statement, a balance sheet, and a cash flow statement.

Once a month actual figures are prepared and compared with budget. Variances (where things are not proceeding according to plan) are highlighted and investigated. Either action is taken to correct actual expenses, e.g., find a cheaper supplier, or the budget itself, and possibly the objectives set, are reconsidered.

As we can see, budgeting causes us to consider the future of the business as defined in objectives and plans. The financial effects of these are calculated so that future cash surpluses or shortfalls can be managed.

Activity

This requires you to carry out a budgetary planning exercise.

The balance sheet of the KRS Company as at 31 August was as follows:

		Fixed assets	Cost	Depreciation	Written-down value
Capital	£27 500				
		Leasehold premises	£20 000	£4000	£16 000
		Fittings	£10 000	£2000	£ 8000
Current liabilities		*Current assets*			
Trade creditors	£ 6000	Stock			£10 000
Bank overdraft	£ 2100	Trade debtors			£ 1600
	£35 600				£35 600

The budgeted figures for the next six months are as follows:

(i) Sales (£)

Sept.	Oct.	Nov.	Dec.	Jan.	Feb.
16 000	16 000	20 000	40 000	12 000	12 000

Some customers are allowed credit and the proportion of cash and credit sales is:

	Cash sales (%)	Credit sales (%)
Nov.	80	20
Dec.	60	40
All other months	90	10

Customers who buy on credit usually pay in the following month.

(ii) Purchases
Purchases have been budgeted as 70 per cent of the sales value, leaving a contribution of 30 per cent. Stocks are maintained by purchasing goods in the month in which they are sold, the exception being December when all goods expected to be sold in January are bought in December. Purchases are paid for in the month following receipt.

(iii) Expenses
Wages have been budgeted at £3000 per month and other expenses at £1000 per month, payment being made in the month incurred.

(iv) Depreciation
Depreciation of leasehold premises and fittings at 10 per cent per annum on original cost.

From the above information, prepare:

1. A cash budget for each of the six months from September to February using the balance sheet as at 31 August as the base.
2. A budgeted profit and loss account for each of these six months.
3. A budgeted balance sheet as at 28 February following these six months.

Below you will find suggested formats for completing these three exercises. We have filled in the first month's figures to give you a start. When you have finished the exercise, compare it with our solution which follows, together with some notes of explanation. The important thing here is to have a go and get the idea of budgeting—it doesn't matter for this exercise whether you get the 'right answer' in every detail. What is important is that you understand the straightforward logic of budgeting which you can apply to your business, your household accounts or even your pocket money.

Suggested formats

1. *Cash budget for the KRS Company*

£	Sept.	Oct.	Nov.	Dec.	Jan.	Feb.
Inflows						
Sales						
Cash	14 400					
Credit	1600					
	16 000					
Outflows						
Purchases	6000					
Wages	3000					
Other expenses	1000					
	10 000					
Net cash flow	6000					
Opening balance	(2000)					
Closing balance	3900					

2. *Budgeted profit and loss account for the KRS Company*

£	Sept.	Oct.	Nov.	Dec.	Jan.	Feb.
Sales	16 000					
Less cost of sales (purchases)	11 200					
Contribution	4800					
Wages	3000					
Expenses	1000					
Depreciation						
Premises	167					
Fittings	83					
Total expenses	4250					
Net profit	550					

3. Budgeted balance sheet for the KRS Company as at 28 February

Capital		Fixed assets	Cost	Depreciation	Written-down value
Profit					
	————	Leasehold			————
	————	premises			————
		Fittings			
Current liabilities					
Trade creditors		*Current assets*			
Bank overdraft		Stock			
	————				————
	————	Trade debtors			————
		Bank			
	————				————
	————				————
	═══════				═══════

Solutions:

1. Cash budget for the KRS Company

£	Sept.	Oct.	Nov.	Dec.	Jan.	Feb.
Inflows						
Sales						
Cash	14 400	14 400	16 000	24 000	10 800	10 800
Credit	1600	1600	1600	4000	16 000	1200
	16 000	16 000	17 600	28 000	26 800	12 000
Outflows						
Purchases	6000	11 200	11 200	14 000	36 400	—
Wages	3000	3000	3000	3000	3000	3000
Other expenses	1000	1000	1000	1000	1000	1000
	10 000	15 200	15 200	18 000	40 400	4000
Net cash flow	6000	800	2400	10 000	(13 600)	8000
Opening balance	(2100)	3900	4700	7100	17 100	3500
Closing balance	3900	4700	7100	17 100	3500	11 500

Explanation. By way of explanation of this cash budget, let's now go through the workings:

	Aug.	Sept.	Oct.	Nov.	Dec.	Jan.	Feb.
(i) Sales (£)	—	16 000	16 000	20 000	40 000	12 000	12 000
Cash		90%	90%	80%	60%	90%	90%
		14 400	14 400	16 000	24 000	10 800	10 800
Credit	1600	1600	1600	4000	16 000	1200	1200
TOTAL	=	16 000	16 000	17 600	28 000	26 800	12 000

The trade debtors' balance in the 31 August balance sheet relates to credit sales in August payable in September. Therefore the monthly credit sales are staggered by one month in the cash budget leaving an outstanding debtor balance at the end of February of £1200.

	Aug.	Sept.	Oct.	Nov.	Dec.	Jan.	Feb.
(ii) Purchases (£)	6000	11 200	11 200	14 000	28 000	—	8400
					8400		
Paid		6000	11 200	11 200	14 000	36 400	—

Purchases are paid for one month after receipt, therefore August purchases are paid in September and so on until February's are outstanding and shown as trade creditors in the balance sheet.

(iii) Wage and other expenses are straightforward, usually wages are one week, or like other expenses, one month in arrears.

(iv) Depreciation is a non-cash transaction and therefore does not appear in the cash budget; only the original purchase or the sale of premises and fittings would feature in the cash flow. However, the assets do lose value, this loss being shown in the profit and loss account.

2. Budgeted profit and loss account for the KRS Company

£	Sept.	Oct.	Nov.	Dec.	Jan.	Feb.	TOTAL
Sales	16 000	16 000	20 000	40 000	12 000	12 000	116 000
Less cost of sales (purchases)	11 200	11 200	14 000	28 000	8400	8400	81 200
Contribution	4800	4800	6000	12 000	3600	3600	34 800
Wages	3000	3000	3000	3000	3000	3000	18 000
Expenses	1000	1000	1000	1000	1000	1000	6000
Depreciation							
Premises	167	167	167	167	167	167	1002
Fittings	83	83	83	83	83	83	498
Total expenses	4250	4250	4250	4250	4250	4250	25 500
Net profit	550	550	1750	7750	(650)	(650)	9300

Explanation.

(i) The difference between net profit and cash flow for each month is represented by the movement in creditors, debtors, stock, and depreciation. This last is a non-cash transaction and is the writing off of an asset over its useful life.

(ii) The difference between net profit and cash flow is quite significant in certain months, for example, September has a profit of only £550 but a net cash inflow of £6000. January's loss is £650, but the net cash outflow is £13 600. This illustrates the crucial difference between the two and shows why adverse cash flows bring so many businesses to grief.

3. *Budgeted balance sheet for the KRS Company as at 28 February*

Capital	27 500	Fixed assets	Cost	Depreciation	Written-down value
Profit	9300				
	36 800	Leasehold premises	20 000	5002	14 998
		Fittings	10 000	2498	7502
					22 500
Current liabilities					
Trade creditors	8400	*Current assets*			
Bank overdraft	—	Stock			10 000
	8400	Trade debtors			1200
		Bank			11 500
					£22 700
	£45 200				£45 200

Explanation. The capital of the KRS Company has increased by £9300, which is the net profit made in the last six months. The bank overdraft of August is now a cash surplus of £11 500. The stock figure has remained as it was and there has been a reduction in the written-down value of the fixed assets. The revised trade creditor and debtor figures reflect the position at the end of February.

FOLLOW-UP

Within work organizations, the task of compiling budgets is usually the responsibility of expert accountants. However, it is important for all managers to possess basic budgetary skills.

If you managed a good try at this activity, then you might wish to graduate to more complex exercises, incorporating, for example, purchases of equipment, sales of vehicles, discounts, loans, loan repayments, etc. Now that you have ability in this area, is it being fully used in your job? If not, how could you begin to use this knowledge?

If, on the other hand, you found this activity difficult, you might be tempted to tell yourself that it doesn't matter—that your job has no budgeting responsibility. But who does prepare the budgets for your department? Do you have access to the organization's master budgets and do you understand them? It is difficult for anyone to manage these days without a firm grasp of 'the bottom line' in any undertaking, and how this is arrived at.

If you want to follow up this activity, there are a number of easily available sources. The best of all is likely to be the accountant in your organization since this person will understand both the master budget and that of your department. Failing this you can try your colleagues, for some of them will certainly have acquired skills in this area. You may also be able to obtain guidance from your local college of further education either by enrolling on a course, or by consulting specialist staff.

Successful budgeting in a Week by Malcolm Secrett (Headway/British Institute of Management, 1993) is an easy introduction in less than 100 pages. John Arnold and Tony Hope's *Accounting for Management Decisions* (Prentice-Hall, 2nd edn, 1990) looks at the subject from the accountant's viewpoint, while *Accounting in a Business Context* by Aidan Berry and Robin Jarvis (Chapman & Hall, 1991) refreshingly takes the perspective of the users of financial data and accounts.

Activity 19
Asserting yourself

Activity

In the following questionnaire, you will find 10 sets of three statements, like this:

I'm a person who

(a) has my rights violated;

(b) protects my own rights;

(c) violates the rights of others.

The scoring is based on the notion that we all behave in each of these ways from time to time, although the extent to which we have a tendency for (a), (b) or (c) will vary.

You are therefore asked to allocate points of each of (a), (b), and (c), such that the total adds up to 10. Thus, if you think that you quite often have your rights violated, and quite often protect the rights of others, but rarely violate the rights of others, you might score yourself as a person who:

(a) has my rights violated;	4
(b) protects my own rights;	4
(c) violates the rights of others.	2
	10

On the other hand, if you recognize that you protect your own rights at all costs, even if this quite often involves violating the rights of others, then your score might be that you are a person who:

(a) has my rights violated;

(b) protects my own rights;

(c) violates the rights of others.

0
6
4
10

Now complete the questionnaire.

I'm a person who:

1. (a) has my rights violated;

    (b) protects my own rights;

    (c) violates the rights of others.

10

2. (a) does not achieve my goals;

    (b) achieves my goals without hurting other people;

    (c) achieves my goals at the expense of other people.

10

3. (a) feels frustrated and unhappy;

    (b) feels good about myself;

    (c) is defensive and/or belligerent.

10

4. (a) is inhibited and withdrawn;

   (b) is socially and emotionally expressive;

   (c) is explosive, hostile, angry.

   10

5. (a) feels hurt, anxious;

   (b) is quietly self-confident;

   (c) is brashly confident, boastful.

   10

6. (a) fails to achieve my goals;

   (b) tries to find ways so that I can achieve my goals
       and others can achieve theirs;

   (c) is not concerned about others and their goals.

   10

7. (a) is gullible, easily taken in;

   (b) is open-minded and questioning;

   (c) is suspicious, cynical.

   10

8. (a) feels bad about my weaknesses;

   (b) is aware of my weaknesses, but don't dislike myself because of them;

   (c) is unaware of my weaknesses.

10

9. (a) allows others to choose for me;

   (b) chooses for myself;

   (c) intrudes on other people's choices.

10

10. (a) is taken advantage of;

    (b) protects my own rights;

    (c) takes advantage of others.

10

This questionnaire is based on a model that suggests that ASSERTION is the 'happy medium' between two equally undesirable extremes—*passivity* and *aggression*. To see where you are, add up all your (a) scores (*passivity*), (b) scores (ASSERTION), and (c) scores (*aggression*), and enter them in the diagram below.

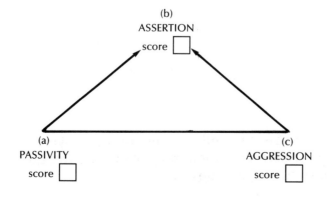

This way of looking at assertion is very important. While it is easy to distinguish it from the left extreme of passivity, it is quite often mistaken and confused with the right extreme of aggression. In fact, though, as the questionnaire statements show, they are very different.

Learning to be assertive requires a lot of practice. You have taken an important step by getting an idea of your passive/assertive/aggressive profile. (Incidentally, why not get others to fill it out for you—to give you *their* picture of where you are?) The (b) behaviours give you an idea of what to aim for if you want to become more assertive; these can become the basis of your intentions for actions. Perhaps you can keep a diary of how assertive you have been from time to time; do certain situations or people tend to push you into passivity or aggression? What is there about these? What can you do about them?

Incidentally, this 'happy medium' way of looking at things can be applied to all sorts of aspects of yourself. For example, are you lazy and slothful? Or a narrow-minded workaholic, burning yourself out? Or purposefully committed, balancing work and leisure?

or again,

No doubt you can think of some of these 'syntheses' as Roberto Assagioli calls them, whereby opposite negative qualities are transformed into positive ones.

FURTHER READING

There are lots of books on assertiveness. *Assertiveness: The Right to be You* by Claire Walmsley (BBC, 1991) is a concise, down-to-earth, self-help book which deals with assertiveness in the home and family as well as at work. Ken and Kate Back's *Assertiveness at Work: A Practical Guide to Handling Awkward Situations* (McGraw-Hill, 1990) is a well-regarded book, as is Anne Dickson's *A Woman in Your Own Right* (Quartet Books, 1982).

Activity 20
Response to conflict

LEARNING AREAS: SOCIAL SKILLS: Emotional resilience: Sensitivity to
events

Some of the important parts of a manager's job are concerned with
conflict. You may be called upon to mediate between two individuals in conflict. You may be in conflict yourself with another
manager who is competing for the same resources or for the ear of a
manager at a higher level. You will be continually handling crises—
unforeseen events caused by breakdowns, absenteeism, loss of
supplies, lack of buyers, and so on.

All these are conflict situations where one party is frustrating the
goals of another party and yet they are dependent on each other.
The outcomes can be many and varied, from outright battling
through negotiations and compromise, to walk-overs or avoidance.
In particular situations one response might be more appropriate
than another, but no one response is correct every time.

Stop and think about your own response tendency to conflict
situations. How do you generally react when faced with frustration
and antagonism? This activity aims to get you to look at your habitual
or preferred response to conflict situations. It also asks you to
generate alternatives to these habitual responses.

The more aware you are of your personal style, and the more ways
you see of being able to resolve a particular conflict, the more
sensitive, flexible, and successful you will be in coping with the
problem.

There are three parts to this activity. Part 1 consists of three short
case studies which invite you to place yourself in particular conflict
situations. Part 2 contains a simple model of conflict resolution
styles and asks you to classify yourself within the model. Part 3 is a
paired comparison questionnaire which provides another way of
examining your preferred approach to resolving conflict. Taken

together, the three parts will build up a picture of the way you react in conflict situations, and provide a basis for more appropriate responses. Each part is complete in itself and can be tackled separately from the others.

Activity. Part 1: Three case studies

After each of the three short case studies, write down what your first reaction would be to that situation. Think yourself into the situation and feel the anger and frustration well up inside you.

Case 1

You have just arrived at the canteen and are waiting for your coffee. Across the room you see a fellow manager with whom you got into a row at the last management meeting. The argument concerned the shortage of skilled clerical staff—you believe your department is failing to get its fair share and that your colleague's is overstaffed. This morning one of your departmental secretaries failed to report for work and on applying to the pool you were told that the last of the 'temps' had gone to your fellow manager's department. At the sight of this person, your anger and sense of injustice flood back.

What do you do? (Write down your first reaction.)

Case 2

The road you live on has a fringe of lawn between the footpath and the road. You look after your section and like to see it looking green and well tended. Most of your neighbours do the same, but on one side of you live some people you don't know too well and who ignore this common policy. They never cut the verge and they and their friends frequently park their cars on it. Recently, they have been parking on your section and, in the recent wet weather, tyre marks marred the green surface. You have spoken to them twice about this, but they appear off-hand and indifferent to your concern. One Sunday morning you wake up at 5 a.m. to the revving of engines, and on looking outside see two deep scars across your lawn.

At 9 o'clock and still seething, you bump into your neighbour in the papershop.

What do you do? (Write down your first reaction.)

Case 3

You are a junior manager in the sales section of a very large company. Your boss sends for you one morning and you hear on the grapevine that you are going to be asked to take on an unpopular duty that involves coming in every other Saturday. You don't like it—you like to keep your weekends free for the family, and you feel you are getting a raw deal because you are junior. You're on your way to the boss's office.

What do you do? (Write down your first reaction.)

When you've responded to these three cases go back over them and see if you can think of *alternative* approaches.

Case 1. Alternative approaches

Case 2. Alternative approaches

Case 3. Alternative approaches

One of the consequences of conflict is that it leads to stress, the hardening of attitudes, and a tendency to be rigid. This is why we have habitual ways of reacting to conflict situations.

- Looking back over your initial reactions to the three cases, can you spot a habitual mode of response?
- Think of conflicts you have had in the past with your spouse, colleagues, parents, etc. Do these show any pattern of response?
- Of the three cases, how many alternatives to each of your initial responses could you generate? Two? Three? Four? Or more?

The more alternatives you generated to each situation the more likely you are to behave flexibly in practice.

Part 2: A conflict style model

Figure A20.1 shows five conflict-resolving models or styles. These are arrived at from the two basic dimensions of conflict situations. In any conflict between two parties the mode of resolution depends upon:

(a) how assertive or unassertive each party is in pursuing its own goals;
(b) how cooperative or uncooperative each party is in pursuing the goals of the other.

If both parties are highly assertive with regard to their own goals and uncooperative in terms of each other's goals then they will adopt a

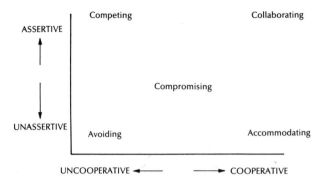

Figure A20.1

battling, *competing* style which is sometimes typical of union/ management negotiations and husband/wife arguments. If the parties are unassertive of their own goals and still uncooperative, they will tend to avoid the conflict altogether and try to pretend it doesn't exist.

What often happens is that parties adopt different styles or modes of resolution in a particular conflict. This will then produce a joint mode which lies between any of the five polar modes on the graph. Resolving conflict is an interactive situation in which styles are mutually reciprocal. The style you adopt will affect the style your opponent adopts, and vice versa.

Try using Fig. A20.1 to diagnose a particular conflict situation in which you have personally been involved. (A personal relationship offers most scope.) Can you fit the adopted modes of the two parties on the chart, and arrive at a description of the joint style of resolution?

Do this with as many conflict situations as you can think of. Research suggests that the appropriate style of resolving conflicts varies with such contingent issues as power, urgency, and specificity of goal. However, by diagnosing your habitual responses in certain situations and observing the responses these produce in others, you can obtain a clearer picture of yourself.

When do you avoid conflict?
When do you compete with others?
Do you ever collaborate in conflict situations?
How do you feel when you accommodate to others?
How often do you secure compromises?

The clearer you can identify your own style(s) and the responses generated in others, the more alternatives you can see in any particular situation, and the more likely you are to behave appropriately the next time conflict arises.

Part 3: Conflict management questionnaire

This questionnaire is designed to help you further identify your preferred style of conflict resolution.

Choose from 30 pairs of statements the one in each case which best fits your preferred style of handling differences between you and others:

1. 1. I am usually firm in pursuing my goals.
   2. I attempt to get all concerns and issues immediately out in the open.
2. 1. I put my cards on the table and invite the other person to do likewise.
   2. When conflicts arise I try to win my case.
3. 1. Once I adopt a position I defend it strongly.
   2. I prefer not to argue but to look for the best solution possible.
4. 1. I sometimes sacrifice my own wishes for the wishes of the other person.
   2. I feel that differences are not always worth worrying about.
5. 1. I accept the views of the other, rather than rock the boat.
   2. I avoid people with strong views.
6. 1. I like to cooperate with others and follow their ideas.
   2. I feel that most things are not worth arguing about. I stick to my own views.
7. 1. I try to find some compromise situation.
   2. I am usually firm in pursuing my goals.
8. 1. When conflicts arise I try to win my case.
   2. I propose a middle ground.
9. 1. I like to meet the other person half-way.
   2. Once I adopt a position I defend it strongly.
10. 1. I feel that differences are not always worth worrying about.
    2. I try to find a compromise solution.
11. 1. I propose a middle ground.
    2. I avoid people with strong views.
12. 1. I feel that most things are not worth arguing about. I stick to my own views.
    2. I like to meet the other person half-way.
13. 1. I am usually firm in pursuing my goals.
    2. I sometimes sacrifice my own wishes for the wishes of the other person.
14. 1. I accept the views of the other, rather than rock the boat.
    2. When conflicts arise I try to win my case.

15. 1. Once I adopt a position I defend it strongly.
    2. I like to cooperate with others and follow their ideas.
16. 1. I try to find a compromise solution.
    2. I sometimes sacrifice my own wishes for the wishes of the other person.
17. 1. I accept the views of the other, rather than rock the boat.
    2. I propose a middle ground.
18. 1. I like to meet the other person half-way.
    2. I like to cooperate with others and follow their ideas.
19. 1. I feel that differences are not always worth worrying about.
    2. I am usually firm in pursuing my goals.
20. 1. When conflicts arise I try to win my case.
    2. I avoid people with strong views.
21. 1. I feel that most things are not worth arguing about. I stick to my own views.
    2. Once I adopt a position I defend it strongly.
22. 1. I attempt to get all concerns and issues immediately out in the open.
    2. I feel that differences are not always worth worrying about.
23. 1. I avoid people with strong views.
    2. I put my cards on the table and invite the other person to do likewise.
24. 1. I prefer not to argue but to look for the best solution possible.
    2. I feel that most things are not worth arguing about. I stick to my own views.
25. 1. I attempt to get all concerns and issues immediately out in the open.
    2. I try to find a compromise solution.
26. 1. I put my cards on the table and invite the other person to do likewise.
    2. I propose a middle ground.
27. 1. I prefer not to argue but to look for the best solution possible.
    2. I like to meet the other person half-way.
28. 1. I sometimes sacrifice my own wishes for the wishes of the other person.
    2. I attempt to get all concerns and issues immediately out in the open.
29. 1. I put my cards on the table and invite the other person to do likewise.
    2. I accept the views of the other, rather than rock the boat.
30. 1. I like to cooperate with others and follow their ideas.
    2. I prefer not to argue but to look for the best solution possible.

SCORING

The questionnaire consists of three statements measuring each of the five conflict-resolving styles discussed above. Each statement is paired in comparison with one statement from each of the other four styles.

The key below shows you how to score your questionnaire. A, B, C, D, and E represent the five conflict-resolving styles as follows:

A = Avoiding
B = Accommodating
C = Compromising
D = Competing
E = Collaborating.

So, for example, if you chose the second statement of the first pair then you would score 1 for E. If you chose the first statement of the second pair you would score another 1 for E, and so on (Table A20.1).

Statement pair	Conflict resolution mode				
	A	B	C	D	E
1				1	2
2				2	1
3				1	2
4	2	1			
5	2	1			
6	2	1			
7			1	2	
8			2	1	
9			1	2	
10	1		2		
11	2		1		
12	1		2		
13		2		1	
14		1		2	
15		2		1	
16		2	1		
17		1	2		
18		2	1		
19	1			2	
20	2			1	
21	1			2	
22	2				1
23	1				2
24	2				1
25			2		1
26			2		1
27			2		1
28		1			2
29		2			1
30		1			2
TOTALS					

Table A20.1

The maximum score for any mode is 12 and the total aggregate score is 30. A score of more than 6 on any mode would indicate a preference for that mode, while a score of less than 6 would indicate relative neglect.

Clearly this is a one-point-in-time measure of your reaction to conflict situations, and should not be treated as having great validity. The best way to use it is to see it as a corroborative device for your own perception of your preferred style and the results you got from the cases earlier in this exercise.

If all three of these—your perception, responses to the cases, and the questionnaire score—point in the same direction then a conclusion is comparatively simple. More uneven results will require puzzling out. As usual other people's opinions are useful additional data—particularly those with whom you have been in conflict!

FOLLOW-UP

You need practice and application if you are to develop further your skills in resolving conflicts.

The ideas on assertiveness and assertiveness training have a bearing on how you orient yourself to conflict situations. Try Activity 19 'Asserting Yourself'. If you are one of those people who think that conflict is intrinsically wrong, and has no part in the ideal organization, you might like to consider the theoretical argument that conflict is a natural part of the checks and balances of organizational life, that organizations hold a balance in a 'pluralistic' situation where there are many or several legitimate interests and priorities that have to live together, rather than some overarching common goal that ought to unite us all. We may be better managers if we accept that conflict and 'politics' are part of organizational life, rather than symptoms of organizational ill health—though there may still be a difference between constructive and destructive conflict and politics. The managerial skill may be in getting the right kind.

Dealing with Difficult People by Roberta Cava (Piatkus, 1990) has mini-cases and sensible suggestions for many types of problem. *Hidden Conflict in Organisations: Uncovering Behind-the-scenes Disputes* edited by Deborah Kolb and Jean Bartunek (Sage Publications, 1992) contains nine articles on social and personal conflicts not usually dealt with in management books.

However, the best way to learn will be from your own experiences. Activities such as 'Personal Journal' (Activity 6) and 'Analysis of Experiences' (Activity 16) are designed to help you learn in this way and could well be applied to conflict experiences.

Activity 21
Practising new group behaviours

LEARNING AREAS: SOCIAL SKILLS: Sensitivity to events: Analytical skills:
Proactivity

Have you ever stopped to think how much of your time at work is spent in groups? Work groups, coffee groups, social groups, project teams, committees for this, that, and the other, probably account for over half your time at work. The needs and demands for increased participation and shared leadership in modern organizations mean that most of us will spend even more time in groups.

How many times have we said . . . 'Oh no! Not another meeting!' We all experience meetings which take up too much of our valuable time; meetings which seem to go round and round in circles and end inconclusively; meetings which produce arguments and bad feelings, meetings which drag on boringly. These are good reasons for taking a critical look at what happens within groups and meetings.

Groups are used for many vital functions—reaching agreements; building consensus on an issue; exchanging information; selling ideas; making decisions; coordinating disparate activities. Unfortunately, what marks many meetings is the little time actually spent on work activity and the large amount of time spent on fighting, bitching, points-scoring, backscratching, and non-work related behaviour. Often the decision facing a group is a difficult one, perhaps involving members who stand to lose or gain resources or prestige as a result. Sometimes the information to be transmitted is controversial; perhaps, instead of selling ideas, members of the group take up time trying to sell themselves. In these situations, achieving the group objective takes a back seat, gets very blurred— people leaving the meeting ask each other what it was all about.

In situations like this, commonplace in all large organizations, and more of a problem the more 'democratic' an organization becomes,

159

the office historian can be forgiven for reminding us that 'this wouldn't have happened in old so-and-so's day'. Unfortunately 'old so-and-so' doesn't have the solution to the present organizational predicament; that management style has passed away. The dilemma of increased organizational democracy versus the need for efficient management makes group decision making vital. The clear indication for every manager is to learn more about how groups work; how I myself behave in a group situation; the effect this has on others; the effect they have on me. The more we can understand behaviour in groups, the more we can control it and harness it to achieve group goals.

The purpose of this activity is to give you some practice at observing group behaviour and also offers an opportunity to experiment with your own behaviour. The more you use the framework presented here in future meetings and groups, the more you will become aware of your own behavioural tendencies and those of others.

Activity. Part 1: Measuring the contribution rate

As a short and simple exercise to get you started on group observation and analysis, try taking a 'contribution count' at your next meeting. You will need a 10- or 15-minute period for this, when you can concentrate on observing and are not being called on to contribute.

On a sheet of paper write the names or identifying marks for members of the group. For the next 10 to 15 minutes, note each contribution made by every group member by putting a mark beside their names. In the example given in Fig. A21.1 a 'five-barred gate method' was used:

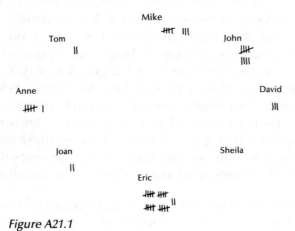

Figure A21.1

A 'contribution' is any spoken comment to the group (not an aside to another member) although it may be directed at one person in particular. It may be short or long, although I often put two marks for a contribution of more than, say, 30 seconds.

In Fig. A21.1 you can see clear differences between the group members in terms of the number of contributions made:

Eric 22 } HIGH contributors
Mike 18

John 9 } MEDIUM contributors
Anne 6

David 3
Tom 2 } LOW contributors
Joan 2
Sheila 0

Now, why did Eric and Mike contribute most? Because they have the most to say, or because they are the more senior? If it was for either of these reasons, their dominance was probably not helping the group move towards its goal. If they spoke most because they knew most about the subject under discussion, or because they were the two principal speakers for and against an idea, then this would probably help the group achieve its goals.

What about David, Tom, Joan, and Sheila? Did they really have nothing to contribute, or were they shut out, asleep, junior, 'unlistened-to' members, or simply not trying?

A contribution count tells you a great deal about a group, especially if you follow it through a number of meetings. The usual pattern is that some members are habitually high contributors and some habitually low and medium, irrespective of the needs of a particular meeting. Behaviour patterns form quickly and we tend to conform to these—although this is done at a subconscious level of which we are not fully aware unless it is brought to our attention.

Share your contribution count with the other members of your group—although you will have to have a very good relationship with them to do this! If a group takes notice of this sort of observation, it can provoke changes in behaviour.

Obviously a contribution count measures only a fraction of what goes on in a group situation, and it should not be taken for more than it is. It takes no account of the *quality* of the contribution; no account of non-verbal behaviour; no account of the requirements of the particular situation; no account of how people are feeling, and so on.

It has the advantage of being an easy thing to do, and it should encourage you to observe and log:

- Who talks to whom. Who do they direct their remarks at and look at when they speak?
- Who interrupts whom?
- Who finally makes the decision—one person, two persons, the whole group?

These are the more difficult to measure, but will give you useful data for your own reflection and, if you can introduce it, for the greater effectiveness of the group.

Part 2: Categorizing behaviour in groups

The effectiveness of groups depends largely upon right behaviour at the right time. When a group is indecisive and bogged down, a clear proposal will often rejuvenate and reorientate it; when several proposals are already on the table, a fresh one will serve to complicate, irritate, and delay. The categories of group behaviour shown in Table A21.1 overleaf have been developed and pioneered in this country by Neil Rackham and have been used to improve group effectiveness by British Airways, International Computers Limited, Rank Xerox International, and many other organizations.

We have chosen just eight categories with which you can practise. There are other categories, but it is confusing and difficult to work with too many. Chose 10- to 15-minute periods in meetings to observe. This will allow concentration and yet not take you right out of the meeting. Use an observation sheet with categories down the left-hand side and group members' names along the top (Table A21.2, p. 164).

Practise on two or four behaviours and two or four people until you get the hang of it. Try logging Mike and Eric on 'proposing', 'giving information', 'seeking information', and 'supporting/building'. High contributors do a lot of proposing and giving information but very little information seeking.

Some generalizations are that groups do a lot of giving—information, proposals, etc., but very little seeking—information, understanding, etc. 'Building' is a rare behaviour and 'summarizing' all too rare. 'Defending/attacking' creates similar responses in others, and a sort of escalation or spiral occurs.

From your observations over a number of meetings and 15-minute periods you should be able to answer some of the following:

Category	Definition
Proposing	—a behaviour which puts forward a new concept, suggestion, or course of action: 'I suggest we call a meeting of all Department employees'.
Giving information	—a behaviour which offers facts, opinions, or clarification to others: 'There is a full definition of this in the handbook'.
Seeking information	—a behaviour which seeks facts, opinions, or clarification from others: 'What do the rest of you think?'
Supporting/building	—a behaviour which declares support or agreement with another person or attempts to extend or develop a proposal made by another person: 'I agree with Sheila and moreover we should start now'.
Disagreeing	—a behaviour which involves a direct criticism, difference of opinion, or disagreement with another person's ideas: 'No my boss would never accept a reduction in his budget'.
Defending/attacking	—a behaviour which attacks another person or defends an individual's own position. More emotional than disagreeing: 'That is a stupid idea' or 'My idea is better than that'.
Blocking/difficulty stating	—a behaviour which blocks another proposal without offering alternatives and without reasons: 'It won't work' or 'We can't have that'.
Testing understanding	—a behaviour which checks and seeks to establish whether an earlier contribution has been understood: 'Can I just ask you, John, did you imply that you were supporting or not supporting Jim's proposal?'
Summarizing	—a behaviour which summarizes, or restates concisely, the content of a previous proposal or discussion: 'Well, so far, ladies and gentlemen, we have heard two proposals: Tom's—to call a meeting immediately; and John's—to delay action until next week'.

Table A21.1

- Do people fall into stereotyped roles? For example, just as there are habitual low contributors so are there chronic proposers who do no supporting and consenters who do no disagreeing?
- Is there a balance of behaviours in the group? For example, people may fall into particular roles, but if these complement each other then the group may function well. Unless somebody *is* doing the summarizing, testing understanding, supporting, etc., several vital functions will be missing.
- How could this group work better? For example, does everybody feel OK about their roles, levels of contribution, and rewards from this group? Does the group make good decisions without undue wasting of time?

Observation sheet		Date					Time		
Names	John	Eric	Mike	Tom	Anne	Sheila	David	Joan	Total
Proposing	II	卌 I	卌		I		I	I	16
Giving information	I	IIII	卌 III	I	II	II	I		I	20
Seeking information	III	I	卌 I	III						
. . . and so on . . .									

Table A21.2

Again, the group could benefit from having your observations fed back to it, but most groups are not used to such self-scrutiny and will tend to reject you, the data, or both. Caution is recommended.

Part 3

You can dispense with some of the caution and be as experimental as you like with your own behaviour. After this observation you will have put together some ideas about the way you behave in groups. Spend some time now summarizing these.

Step 1

What characteristics have you noticed in yourself?

- Are you a medium, low, or high contributor?
- Are you a proposer, a builder, or what?
- How much seeking behaviour do you practise?
- What happened the last time you were in a defending/attacking position?
- How often do you test your understanding of other people's ideas?

Step 2

Choose some of the behaviour you'd like to practise more often; some you'd like to cut back on.

Step 3

At the next meeting you attend, experiment by using one new behaviour. If you're trying to lessen a behaviour, try cutting it out altogether.

Step 4

Observe carefully what effect you're having. You may be able to elicit feedback from people's behaviour towards you in the meeting or by conversations afterwards.

Step 5

If you're stuck for behaviours to try, remember that seeking information, building, summarizing, and testing understanding are often low in groups. Here are some suggested actions.

At the next meeting try one of the following:

- Do nothing but ask questions.
- Never ask a question.
- Do not agree or disagree with anything.
- Each time you're not absolutely sure what another person means, ask for clarification.
- If you're normally a high contributor—say nothing; if you're normally low—aim to say more than anyone else.

FOLLOW-UP

There will always be meetings in which you can observe and experiment. One thing we promise you, if you use these ideas you will never look at a meeting in the same way again. You will notice things that passed you by before.

This type of analysis is described in more detail in *Behaviour Analysis in Training* by Neil Rackham and Terry Morgan (McGraw-Hill, 1977). David Buchanan and Andrej Huczynski's *Organisational Behaviour: An Introductory Text* (Prentice-Hall, 1985) devotes the whole of its second part to behaviour in groups. Sonya Hamlin's *How to Talk So People Will Listen* (Thorsens, 1989) covers meetings, presentations and one-to-one communication, and is a practical book with helpful tips. John Hayes' *Interpersonal Skills: Goal-directed Behaviour at Work* (HarperCollins, 1991) covers a wide range of situations.

Activity 22
Interpreting yourself and others

LEARNING AREAS: SOCIAL SKILLS: Self-knowledge: Analytical skills

The way you behave towards other people, and your success and failure in achieving things with and through other people, depends very much on the extent to which you see them as they see themselves, and you see yourself as they see you.

Every action you take to influence other persons is based on a complex set of conscious or unconscious assumptions about the meaning they will attach to your action and the way in which they will respond to it.

Part 1 of this activity is designed to help you become aware of some of the ways you see other people and yourself.

Part 2 suggests that you check this out in some way to see how your perceptions coincide with those of others.

Activity. Part 1

Step 1

In the boxes in column 1 of Fig. A22.1 write the names of five people with whom you interact frequently in the work context, about things that are important to your work and your organization's functioning.

Step 2

In columns 2 and 3 are further boxes, joined in pairs by horizontal lines. These lines represent dimensions on which people might differ (e.g., aggressive–meek, clever–stupid, honest–devious, etc.) in your mind. Each dimension is joined to two of the name boxes in column 1. Take each 'dimension' in turn and look at the names of the people in the two boxes. Think of a way in which these two

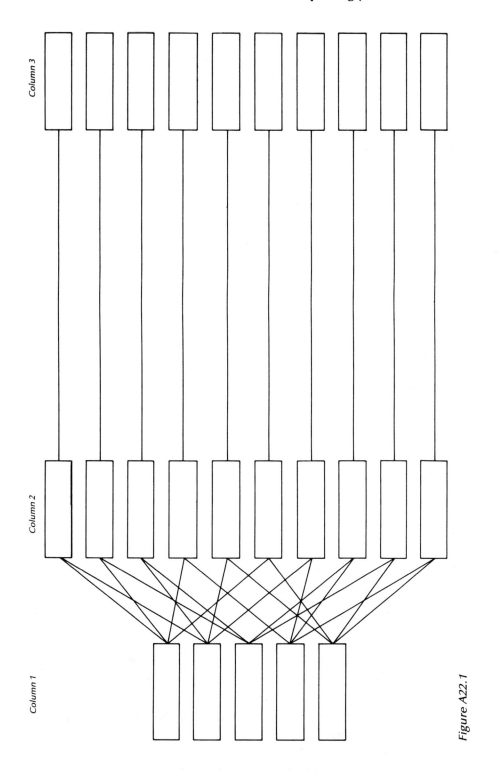

Figure A22.1

people seem different to you, and a pair of words, like quick–slow, funny–serious, reliable–unreliable, to describe that difference. Put one word in the box at each end of the dimension. It does not matter which end you put the words. Do this 10 times, once for each of the dimensions. Try to make sure you find a different dimension each time. It does not matter if you do not account for all, or even the main differences between the two people each time, as long as you get one aspect of it. The idea is to find out the ways in which you classify people.

Step 3

Treating each dimension as a scale, put a cross on it where you think you are, and mark it with your initials. (See Fig. A22.2.)

Figure A22.2

Treat the dimension as a scale from extreme to extreme—e.g., complete reliability to complete unreliability, even if the people who led you to think of it in the first place are not at the extremes.

Part 2

Part 1 should have given you food for thought about yourself in relation to those with whom you work. You can get more from it. Here are some possibilities:

(a) Decide what you would like to be like by ticking the dimensions where you would like to be.
(b) Try *being* different. If you can do so, is it what you really want?
(c) Choose one of the 'five'; mark where you think this person is on each dimension, and show it to him or her, getting a reaction to where you put him or her and yourself.
(d) Do the exercise with one or more of the others, sharing and discussing your conclusions.
(e) As you go about your normal activities, see if you can find ways of checking whether you see others as they see themselves, and whether they see you as you see yourself.

FOLLOW-UP

You will get much more out of this if you involve yourself in getting other people's views. 'Where to go from here' is simply to develop the habit and skill of checking on your perceptions of others, and on how you come across to them.

Activity 23
Counselling style inventory

LEARNING AREAS: SOCIAL SKILLS: Sensitivity to events: Self-knowledge

Much of a manager's time with staff is spent in a listening, receiving posture. The ideal manager is a helper who provides personal support for staff. Leonard Sayles calls this function 'responsiveness' and notes that if a manager is accessible to staff they will often come just to be listened to.[1] Listening is a key managerial skill and one of the aspects which people value most.

In the hectic environment of the work world, there is also the need for action. A manager achieves results through other people working well and some of the most important actions concern the motivation of people. This is rarely a simple 'carrot and stick' exercise, but a complex process requiring a detailed knowledge of the individual needs of staff, and considerable helping skills. Help is not always helpful, however, as all those who have been helped, advised, and put right will know. Deciding what is helpful in a given situation is a skill in itself.

We'll call this listening and helping activity 'counselling'. The following activity will help you to analyse your counselling style.

Activity

Five short paragraphs depict statements from people who might be on your staff, and five sets of five responses to the statements. You are to choose the response which you feel you would most likely make. Be honest with yourself—there are no simple 'right answers'—and you have everything to gain from an honest analysis of your behaviour.

When you have read Situation A turn to the five responses and choose one. Then turn back and read Situation B, and so on.

SITUATION A

Man, aged 35
'I have a lot of ambition. Every job I've had I've been successful at, and I intend to be successful here even if it means walking over a few people to do so. I'm going to prove myself and really go places.'

SITUATION B

Woman, aged 26
'Two years at business school have really equipped me to be a professional manager. Competing with men there has convinced me that women who get as far as I have are more than a match for most men. If this organization wants to keep me it will have to fit in with my own career progression.'

SITUATION C

Man, aged 44
'I used to be very ambitious but, as I've got older, success is not so important to me. I may not have been a success with the company, but I've put all my real effort into my family. I'm a very happy family man.'

SITUATION D

Woman, aged 41
'When I moved to this town I thought I'd make lots of new friends. Being single and living alone I've always had quite a social life.... But it doesn't seem to happen somehow ... the work is fine, but people here aren't interested in socializing much. I think it must be me ... I'm getting more closed up and into myself....'

SITUATION E

Man, aged 32
'I'm telling you, Lewis has really got his knife into me. I got the blame for the whole of the Brown and Williamson affair and there were eight of us involved. Now he's trying to insinuate I'm falling down on the job. I had a good name in this office until he came here—he just doesn't like me and he's determined to do me down.'

SITUATION A	Choose *one* of the following responses:

1. 'You feel you are a very ambitious man, is that right?'
2. 'Why do you think you have such strong needs for success?'
3. 'That's good. You should soon get to the top with that attitude. Let me know if I can help you in any way.'
4. 'It seems to me that your needs for success are so strong that they outweigh your needs to be popular.'
5. 'It will make you very unpopular here if you maintain that attitude, that's not how we do things here at all.'

SITUATION B	Choose *one* of the following responses:

1. 'A business school education is a great asset, but if you ask me it doesn't make you a good manager. You have to learn that the hard way.'
2. 'What difficulties do you foresee in being female in this organization?'
3. 'I'm sure you're right. We are really in need of people with your skills and drive. Let's get together next week and I'll help you plan out how you can get the experience you want in this department in the shortest possible time.'
4. 'If I'm hearing you correctly, you feel that you are well equipped as a professional manager and you expect the organization to respect this?'
5. 'It appears to me that you have some worries about being accorded the status you think you deserve?'

SITUATION C	Choose *one* of the following responses:

1. 'That sounds like a very sensible attitude, after all, very few people get to the top. Is there any help I can give you in this?'
2. 'Yes, you reached the point where you decided to switch goals— from your career to your family—but you feel perhaps that something is missing?'
3. 'You're absolutely right. A man's a fool to keep struggling when nobody cares a damn. You did the right thing and I'd do the same in your position.'
4. 'As you have got older you find more and more satisfaction with your family.'
5. 'Why do you feel that you weren't a success with the company? What do you mean by success?'

| SITUATION D | Choose *one* of the following responses: |

1. 'Can you tell me more about how you go about making friends? Have you made any efforts recently to meet people?'
2. 'Living alone is OK if you have lots of friends, but without them it's very lonely—is that what you're saying?'
3. 'It looks as though you may be really worried about the future, perhaps you've lived alone for so long that you've dropped out of the habit of getting close to people?'
4. 'That sounds really sad, to be lonely and without friends. What you've got to do is get out and about and make some... If I were you I'd get started straight away.'
5. 'Well, let's see... there are lots of ways in which you could get involved with the staff social club. Next month there's the annual outing and I could get you on the organizing team, how would you like that?'

| SITUATION E | Choose *one* of the following responses: |

1. 'You are getting paranoic feelings about Lewis, could it be that you are working out your frustrations at not getting the job you both applied for?'
2. 'You're right, he can really be a mean so-and-so when he chooses, but I wouldn't go about it with your attitude.'
3. 'Are there any other occasions when he's tried to show you up in a poor light?'
4. 'If I understand you correctly, you feel persecuted by Lewis and think that he intends to wreck your reputation?'
5. 'Right, you need to protect yourself from situations like this. Do you know that the union is becoming very strong among our grades, in fact, I've got some application forms here, I'll help you fill them out.'

SCORING

In the grid (Table A23.1), the situations are listed on the left-hand side and the responses (1 to 5) fall into the five categories E, I, S, P, U along the top. Look at the response you selected for each situation and note which letter it falls under. For example, if you chose response 3 to Situation A then you note one 'S'. Do this for all five situations.

RESPONSES

		E	I	S	P	U
S I T U A T I O N S	A	5	4	3	2	1
	B	1	5	3	2	4
	C	3	2	1	5	4
	D	4	3	5	1	2
	E	2	1	5	3	4

Table A23.1

You should now have a score for all five types of responses, e.g., how many Es did you score? how may Is? and so on, for example:

Responses

E	2
I	1
S	2
P	—
U	—
	5

DISCUSSION

This exercise is based on the work of Carl Rogers who developed these five response categories[2] from studies done on face-to-face communication. These categories accounted for 80 per cent of all messages sent between people and generally speaking are used as follows:

E—used most
I—used next most
S—used third most
P—fourth most
U—used least

The categories are as follows:

E—Evaluative response	—making judgements.
I—Interpretative response	—'reading between the lines', making hunches.
S—Supportive response	—agreeing, backing up, offering psychological and actual support.
P—Probing response	—questioning, asking for more, often deeper, information.
U—Understanding response	—understanding is used in a rather special way— it refers to a non-directive, non-evaluative response which reflects back to the speaker what he/she said.

The categories themselves are neither good nor bad. They are more or less appropriate in particular situations.
What is important is that:

1. We tend to have habitual, fixed ways of responding, therefore we over-use some categories and under-use others.

Which categories do you over-use?

Which categories do you under-use?

2. People tend to pigeonhole us—Rogers says that if we use any one response for 40 per cent or more of the time, then *we are always seen as behaving like that.*

Did you score two Es, Is, Ss, Ps, or Us?

If so, you may be seen as being this sort of person. If you scored three or four for one type of response, then you are likely to be using this sort of response consistently. Other people almost certainly have this image of you. Don't forget that there is no right way of behaving for all situations. The purpose of this activity is to highlight your counselling style and illustrate some alternative.

FOLLOW-UP

While we have talked here of counselling style, some people would use the word coaching to describe this sort of reflective listening. In practice there is quite a lot of overlap between the two in the work situation and many of the same skills are involved. If you are interested in Carl Rogers' ideas and want to read him in the original, try his *On Becoming a Person* (Constable, 1971).

John Michael Hughes' *Counselling for Managers: An Introductory Guide* (Bacie, 1991) is exactly that, while David Megginson and Tom Boydell's *A Guide to Management Coaching* (Bacie, 1979) is another good short text containing development activities on both coaching and counselling. Mentoring is another overlapping and related skill. David Clutterbuck's *Everyone Needs a Mentor* (IPM, 2nd edn, 1991) is a useful text.

The John Cleese treatment for coaching in five steps can be seen in *The Helping Hand* (Video Arts, 1990).

A good way of follow-up—as with all managerial skills—is to prac-tise, as often as you can in real situations. Using the framework in this activity you can experiment with new types of responses—try to do more probing or reflecting back. If you are habitually non-directive, be more supportive and evaluative at times.

REFERENCES

1. Sayles, L., *Managerial Behaviour*, McGraw-Hill, 1964, pp. 149–153.
2. Rogers, C. R., *Client-Centred Therapy*, Houghton Mifflin, 1951.

Activity 24
Getting to know you

LEARNING AREAS: SOCIAL SKILLS: Self-knowledge

To get to know somebody well, we have to do more than talk about trivial things. We have to reveal significant aspects of ourselves and of our lives; in turn, the other person is likely to reveal something of him or herself. This mutual process of exchanging personal information leads to better understanding and acceptance of each other.

Everyday social norms, and natural reticence, usually prevent us from talking openly with strangers—even with fairly close acquaintances. This activity is therefore designed in such a way that personal open exchanges are legitimized. It can be used in any situation where you want to get to know somebody else reasonably well, reasonably quickly. At the same time you will find the process of sharing and receiving personal information will increase your level of self-understanding.

Activity

If you are carrying out a self-development programme with a partner (see Chapter 7), this activity is a good way to get started.

Before commencing the activity make sure that each of you *wants* to get to know the other better.

Find a place where you won't be disturbed and set aside at least an hour.

Instructions

Read these instructions carefully before looking at Table A24.1.

You will find a number of incomplete statements. Starting with the first, one of you should complete the statement by telling your partner as much or as little as you want. Your partner can respond to what you say in any way he or she likes. In turn the partner should complete the statement and you can respond in any way you wish. When this process is complete, move on to statement 2, and so on.

Don't look ahead at the other statements—concentrate only on the one being discussed.

Be as revealing as you like—it is entirely up to each person to decide how much to say.

Stop this activity whenever either one of you wishes to do so.

WHEN YOU ARE READY, BEGIN

1. My name is . . .

2. My job is . . .

3. My age is . . .

4. I live . . .

5. I was born in . . .

6. My previous jobs included . . .

7. Things I like best about this job are . . .

8. Things I like least about this job are . . .

9. To me, being a woman/man . . .

10. My marital status is . . .

11. Children . . .

12. My parents . . .

13. My friends . . .

14. My hobbies/spare-time activities . . .

15. When I get to work . . .

16. When I leave work . . .

17. At this very minute, I feel . . .

18. Ideally, this time next year . . .

Table A24.1. The statements

19. In the long term, my ambition . . .

20. The trouble with this organization is . . .

21. My idea of an ideal holiday would be . . .

22. Things that I find very difficult . . .

23. If the worst comes to the worst in 12 months' time . . .

24. The sort of things I worry about . . .

25. What this country needs . . .

26. My religious beliefs . . .

27. To me, being black/white . . .

28. My secret fears . . .

29. My feelings about you . . .

30. My feelings about myself are . . .

Table A24.1. continued

FOLLOW-UP

When you have finished this activity, reflect on it.

How did you feel?

How open and revealing were you?

Were you more open about some types of issue rather than others?

Activity 25
Getting to yes

LEARNING AREAS: SOCIAL SKILLS: Emotional resilience: Sensitivity to events

> Getting to Yes . . . [by Fischer & Ury] . . . is by far the best thing I've ever read about negotiation — J. K. Galbraith

Step 1

Consider the following statements and decide which list — A or B — best describes how you are likely to behave in a negotiation:

A	B
Yield to pressure	Pile on pressure
Make offers	Make threats
Trust others	Distrust others
Search for the single answer, the one they will accept	Hold out for the single answer, the one you will accept

Activity 19, 'Asserting Yourself', looks at the ways we behave with others and categorizes these as passive, aggressive or assertive. Simply put, passive behaviour allows others to walk over us, aggressive behaviour means we walk over others (and their rights), whereas assertive behaviour allows each of us to walk forward.

If we relate this to negotiation, we see that the soft negotiator wants to avoid conflict, and so readily makes concessions to reach agreement. Although wanting an amicable agreement, he or she may end up feeling exploited — just as a habitually passive partner may do in a personal relationship. Similarly, the hard negotiator sees the situation as a contest of wills, in which the side who takes up the most extreme position, shouts loudest and holds out longest, always fares best. Such archetypal aggressive behaviour may yield short-term success, but over time is likely to deplete resources, damage relationships, and exhaust and isolate the protagonist.

Which is most like you — A or B?

There is a third approach, both hard and soft, based on the concept that it is possible to obtain what you are entitled to and still behave decently. Here negotiation is approached and seen as a 'making' process, where all parties build an agreement with which they all can live.

Step 2

The approach here follows that developed at the Harvard Negotiation Project and described in the book *Getting to Yes* by Roger Fischer and William Ury which is explicitly designed to produce agreements which are fair and fully implementable. It is called principled negotiation, or negotiation on merits. There are four principles.

1. Separate the people from the problem
Sort the following statements by soft positional, hard positional, principled negotiation; (you should find two of each):

(a) Proceed independent of trust
(b) Go easy on the people and the problem
(c) On balance, it is best to trust others
(d) Go easy on the people but hard on the problem
(e) Be hard on the people and the problem
(f) On balance, it is best to distrust others

2. Focus on interests, not positions
Explore mutual interests, rather than make offers or issue threats.

3. Invent options for mutual gain
Trying to design good solutions while under pressure is difficult. The presence of an adversary tends to narrow our vision. Our imaginative skills dry up. One way round this is to set aside an agreed period of time in which to develop a wide range of possible solutions that advance *shared interests*.

4. Insist on objective criteria
An aggressive negotiator may try to get their way simply through intransigence. The assertive negotiator can insist that some fair standard is used, such as market value, independent expert advice, law, health and safety regulations, or something similar.

Step 3

Think of a current or forthcoming negotiation. This might be at work—with colleagues over scarce resources, with another department over a shared project—or it might be at home—with a partner over holidays, child care and so on. It is best to think of a situation where the parties have roughly equal power—negotiation between 'bosses' and 'subordinates' has a different flavour.

Thinking of this negotiation, use the four principles to analyse it. Fill in any ideas you have for ways in which you can apply principled negotiation to the situation you have in mind. You may find it useful to do this with a friend.

1 Separate the people from the problem	2 Focus on interests not positions	3 Invent options for mutual gain	4 Insist on objective criteria

Step 4

Preparation is always important for good negotiation. Find time to develop your ideas before you come face-to-face with the other party. If you are part of a team or with colleagues who will be accompanying you, set aside some time to brainstorm the options for mutual gain. This is good preparation in more than one sense, for it will often develop a sense of unity and team. Of course, you're not trying to reach firm decisions in advance of working with the other party or parties—just letting the possibilities see the light of day.

FOLLOW-UP

This activity is based on *Getting to Yes: Negotiating agreement without giving in* by Roger Fischer and William Ury (Arrow Books, 1982) which is about the best you can find in this field. Claire Walmsley's *Assertiveness: the right to be you* (BBC Books, 1991) is a well-designed book with lots of useful ideas at the personal level. John Carlisle and Bob Parker's *Beyond Negotiation* (Wiley, 1989) is about building cooperation in the context of buyer–supplier re-lationships and is again full of useful ideas and processes.

Activity 26
Collaborative working

The 'task force' has long been part of the management repertoire, and as project management it has assumed new importance in recent years. Organizations are increasingly involved in joint ventures, collaborative projects and inter-agency working. These all involve pooling resources, concentrating expertise and bringing together energy and effort across departmental and organizational boundaries. However, such projects have their difficulties, especially when much of the planning and preparation goes into the technical side—design of the task, finance and budgets and so on. Often little thought is given to the social, the interpersonal, the political with a small p.

The project approach places a premium on collaborative working. People find themselves working with or managing people for whom they don't have routine responsibility and perhaps have little contact with again. You might find yourself spending a couple of days a week seconded to another part of the company or to a new, temporary organization because of your expertise, or because no-one else is available. There may be a conflict between your loyalties to your department and to the project team which pulls you one way and then the other. The project can be simple or complex; very concrete and time-specific, such as installing a new computer system by a set date, or it may start with only a generalized goal, such as thinking through the implications of a new product or service. Top management's approach to the project may be highly directive and supervisory, or it may be hands-off, letting the project team generate its own momentum and way of working, and so on.

For this kind of collaboration to be effective, certain 'rules of engagement' need to be established. Otherwise, resentments, lack of cooperation and incomplete development of the project may follow. Often it is the apparently simple and practical issues of

183

working together which cause project teams to fail. Lack of clarity as to what to expect of each other can cause tension and frustration.

The following activity is to help you prepare for collaborative working. It works best if you relate it to a specific project in which you are about to be involved.

The activity

Step 1

List all the things that you would be prepared to share in a collaborative working relationship.

Here's the start of a list which you can add to or delete from:

1. office space
2. secretarial facilities
3. computer access
4. your files
5. your ideas
6. your phone
7. your favourite lunch venue
8. other

You could add certain provisos—'will share office as long as it's left tidy'.

Now make a list of the things you would *not* be willing to share— again, you might want to move things from this list on to the 'share' list, and to add items not mentioned:

1. your professional networks and contacts
2. your books
3. your departmental budget
4. your time outside work
5. other

Step 2

What worries have you about this project?

Take time to jot these down, (e.g., extra workload? concerns about members of the project team having to rely on each other a lot?

getting other managers' cooperation? risks to your reputation? worries about disclosing know-how or information? having to manage the rest of your work as well as the project?).

Step 3

Collaborative working can be a powerful learning opportunity. What learning goals could you accomplish via this project?

Here are a few possible examples to start you off.

1. To widen my knowledge outside my professional field
2. To increase my visibility with senior people
3. To gain experience of other parts of the company/industry
4. To put myself into a high-risk situation
5. To improve my group working and management skills
   and so on.

Now think about what you could *offer* to others in this collaborative work. Arguably, in self-development terms, being able to offer knowledge, skills and personal qualities is as important as being able to acquire what you need. What would you like to offer to others on this project in terms of:

• knowledge?
• skills?
• personal qualities?

Step 4

Next think about the qualities you would like in project colleagues. Complete the following sentences:

What I want are people who *know* _____

What I want are people who *can* _____

What I want are people who *will* _____

You might like to include standards of behaviour in this list. How should this person behave towards your staff, your boss, yourself? What are the actions likely to provoke resentment (e.g., borrowing things without asking, not listening to suggestions, using offensive language)? While you are at it, is there any way you might need to moderate or change you own behaviour?

Step 5

Finally, draft a simple agreement in plain terms covering how you and the others can work together. You could discuss your ideas and concerns with someone who will give you sensible feedback, and you could suggest that your collaborators go through a similar exercise before you meet to discuss these matters.

FOLLOW-UP

The Little Black Book of Project Management by Michael C. Thomsett (American Management Association, 1990) is a readable and well-organized guide to the practicalities of project management. Mark Brown's *Successful Project Management in a Week* (Headway/ British Institute of Management, 1992) is short and concise, while on Dennis Lock's *Project Management* (Gower, 4th edn, 1988) has become a standard text strong on scheduling and financial aspects. For a wider view of how the world of work is changing in these terms try Rosabeth Moss Kantor's 'The New Managerial Work' in *Management of Change* (Harvard Business Review paperback, 1991).

Activity 27
Looking after yourself

LEARNING AREAS: EMOTIONAL RESILIENCE: Self-knowledge

Stress-related diseases are now the main killers of managers and professional workers between the ages of 35 and 64. Heart disease alone accounts for more than a quarter of a million deaths in England. A hundred years or so ago, we were learning that the inhalation of dust and fumes led to lung disease and silicosis. We are now learning what causes coronary heart disease, cancer, and strokes. It is increasingly obvious that these diseases are related to the way we live and work—which includes what we eat, how much we exercise, how much tension and pressure we experience, and how we handle our emotions and feelings.

Looking after ourselves is not just about avoiding an early grave, though this should be motive enough. The killers—heart disease and cancer—head an unpleasant list of usually non-fatal ailments which include arthritis, asthma, chronic anxiety, colitis, diabetes, eczema, hypertension, mental illness, neurosis, migraines and many other symptoms of physical, emotional, and mental distress.

So how do you feel so far? This is not a pretty picture and it's one to which we are surprisingly ready and able to close our eyes. This activity starts with a short questionnaire on how you behave at work.

Activity

Step 1. Work habits questionnaire

How are you at work? Relaxed, tolerant and easy-going? Or are you tense, easily frustrated and irritable? Ring the number on each scale that best characterizes your *usual* response or behaviour at work, i.e., 1 or 5 if you are *very* like the behaviour described at that end; 2 or 4 if you lean towards that end; and 3 if you genuinely feel in the middle.

1. . . . am uncompetitive, 1 2 3 4 5 . . . am highly competitive,
   avoid conflict   I like battles

2. . . . do things at   1 2 3 4 5 . . . do things quickly,
   an easy pace   (walk, eat, drive, etc.)

3. . . . feel as though   1 2 3 4 5 . . . feel as though there's
   there's always   never enough time
   plenty of time

4. . . . have many   1 2 3 4 5 . . . am only interested
   hobbies and   in work, I talk a lot
   interests   about work

5. . . . always do one   1 2 3 4 5 . . . usually keep
   thing at a time   several balls in the
                           air at once

6. . . . never hurry   1 2 3 4 5 . . . am always rushing
                          about, always in a hurry

7. . . . take time off   1 2 3 4 5 . . . feel guilty about
   to relax and   taking time off to
   to think things   relax
   over

8. . . . am casual   1 2 3 4 5 . . . am never late
   about timekeeping

TOTAL SCORE...................(sum of all the ringed numbers)

This questionnaire is based upon the work of two heart specialists, Drs Friedman and Rosenman (1974) who suggest that certain types of behaviour are much more likely to lead to coronary heart disease. A composite of these behaviours gives us the 'Type A' person who is:

- very competitive;
- continually striving for achievement;
- for ever in a hurry;
- liable to explosive outbursts of 'free floating aggression';
- tense, pressurized, urgent, 'hyped up'.

By contrast, the 'Type B' person is:

- relaxed;
- able to play without guilt;
- able to become absorbed in books, entertainments, conversations, and other non-work interests;
- not easily irritated, frustrated or angered;
- in little need of displaying achievements.

So how did you score? If you scored between:

8 and 15	then you're a definite 'Type B' person;
16 and 23	then you lean towards the 'Type B' person;
exactly 24	then you're well balanced between the two;
25 and 32	then you lean towards 'Type A';
33 and 40	they you're definitely 'Type A'.

An absolute 'Type B' person would be so 'laid back' that managing as an activity would either be impossible or not worth the trouble! The important point is that much managerial and professional work reinforces any natural tendencies we have and actually *requires* 'Type A' behaviours. We are rewarded for displaying them. This is the main way in which managerial and professional work forms us — or rather, deforms us.

So, what can we do about this?

Step 2. *Healthy habits*

Here are some ways of avoiding the worst effects of managerial work and of building up inner strength. Tick any of these that you do habitually and add any of your own to the bottom.

1. I build up resistance by regular sleep, a healthy diet and plenty of exercise. [ ]
2. I talk problems through with my spouse. [ ]
3. I talk problems through with my boss or colleagues. [ ]
4. I practise meditating or relaxation. [ ]
5. I withdraw physically from stressful situations when I can. [ ]
6. I block out one day or half day per month in my diary just to spend exactly as I want. [ ]
7. I allow myself a good read every day with a novel that takes all my attention. [ ]
8. I give myself breaks and treats when I need them. [ ]
9. I practise being quiet and avoiding the centre of attention. [ ]
10. [ ]
11. [ ]
12. [ ]
etc.

SCORE one point for each of 1 to 9 that you ticked; SCORE two points for each of 10 onwards.

If you scored more than seven points than you may get stressed up on occasions, but at least you do have some ways of giving yourself a break now and then. If you scored less than seven points, don't you think you should be doing something about this? Perhaps you could start with the next two activities in this book—'Relaxation' and 'Fitness'.

Step 3

As you may have discovered by now, the secret of managing stress successfully is by being able to 'pleasure' yourself without guilt. Does that sound a bit self-indulgent? Even not quite decent? Well, that is a problem. The Victorian work ethic encouraged people to split off their enjoyment and pleasures in life and keep them apart from the stern rectitude and selfless duty required at work. They also knew, better than us, it seems, how a little secrecy intensifies pleasure! Nevertheless, many of us seem to have inherited some guilt about enjoying ourselves at work. Yet there is nothing incompatible about enjoyment and productivity.

If we want to work hard and continue to enjoy rather than to destroy ourselves, we need to take our pleasures seriously!

Treats

Treats are the rewards and gifts you give yourself. 'I'll just have a little something now' you say, and quite right too. Being able to treat yourself is having the ability to reward and pamper yourself at appropriate times—at the end of a hard day, in the middle of a knotty problem, when all seems gloomy and hopeless. Treats are usually little things that give great pleasure—a long hot bath, a walk in the park during office hours, picking or buying flowers for yourself and so on.

Now write down at least five ways in which you treat yourself:

1.
2.
3.
4.
5.

Did you manage that? If you didn't, perhaps you could do some research among your friends or colleagues. This is good fun and throws up a surprising catch—washing dishes in lovely warm water, listening to the Archers in bed on Sundays, ironing while watching TV, getting up early and having the house to yourself, wearing an old and treasured garment. There are all sorts of possibilities.

Incidentally, if you couldn't think of five ways in which you treat yourself then you're probably of the male gender. Men are notoriously bad at treating themselves—'real men' surely don't use bubble bath! (do they?) and many men have grown up relying on women to be the 'emotional specialists' and make them feel better at the end of a hard day in the office, etc. Well, they'd better start learning to do it for themselves (though this does not exclude pleasuring others—on the contrary, being able to treat oneself *increases* one's general ability to give pleasure to others), before it's too late. On average men die eight years earlier than women.

FOLLOW-UP

There are now many books around on managing stress. You could start with Cary Cooper's *The Stress Check* (Prentice-Hall, 1981). *Managing Pressure at Work* by Helen Froggatt and Paul Stamp (BBC Books, 1991) includes worksheets and checklists and is good on making the most of the positive aspects of stress and minimizing negative stress. *Pressure at Work: A Survival Guide* by Tanya Arroba and Kim James (McGraw-Hill, 1987) is another useful workbook which helps you to deal with stress in others and in the organization as well as in yourself.

REFERENCES

Friedman, M. and R. H. Rosenman, *Type A Behaviour and your Heart,* Wildwood House, London, 1974.

Activity 28
Relaxation

LEARNING AREA: EMOTIONAL RESILIENCE

When we first evolved, we were constantly faced with threats in the form of dangerous animals, warring bands, and so on. The reaction to these threats was to get rid of them—either directly by fighting them, or indirectly by fleeing from them.

To help with these reactions the human body (like that of animals) prepared itself in various ways. These include an increased rate of breathing, a raised blood pressure, faster heart beats, greater flow of blood to muscles, and a number of other complex and inter-related physiological responses.

Today's managers, seldom faced with danger from wild beasts, find themselves in a number of threatening situations. In the course of the job they become involved in deals, with conflicts, in meeting difficult deadlines, in making decisions with inadequate infor-mation. They will negotiate, confront, take risks. Often—increasingly so these days—their own job security may seem to be in considerable doubt.

Although the types of stressful situation that the manager faces are very different from those of our ancestors, the body's response is identical. In these situations there are marked increases in pulse rate, blood pressure, breathing, etc.

Unfortunately, these body responses—while excellent for prepar-ing us either to fight a wild beast or to run as fast as possible—don't help us to cope with managerial problems. Furthermore, as we usually don't actually fight or run, all the physiological changes have to be channelled into other effects.

Some of these, particularly in the short term, can be seen as displaced fight or flight behaviour. Shouting or snapping irritably is a form of flight. If we are frightened of our boss, we may 'fight' someone with less power to retaliate, such as member of our staff, spouse, or child. Flight behaviour can be seen in numerous forms, including never-ending attempts to change jobs, day-dreaming, putting vast energies into tackling other problems (which are in fact much easier, even trivial), and headaches and other elusive but painful symptoms that give us the socially acceptable escape route of being 'off colour', going home early, or staying home ill.

In the longer term, the body's responses to stressful and threatening situations are gradually to build up, with very real and serious consequences, the conditions that lead to heart attacks, strokes, ulcers, colitis.

One way of coping with the more immediate physical symptoms of stress is by taking tranquillizers. However, these can hardly be recommended as a long-term solution; what is needed is an internal method of coping with stress reactions.

In recent years a number of such internal methods have grown in popularity. There are often associated with specific cults, philosophies, or religions. Yoga is a well-known approach; transcendental meditation is another.

The activity suggested here is not associated with any particular cult or belief system, but is based on a synthesis of the common elements of a number of approaches to relaxation. More than with most of the activities in this book, you need to repeat this activity over a longish period of time for it to work at its best.

Activity

Step 1

Find a quiet place where you can sit down comfortably. It is important to be fairly straight and upright. Although some people like to sit cross-legged on the floor, this is not essential and you may be more comfortable in a chair. In this case sit with both feet on the ground, back straight, head up. Don't be *too* comfortable—you mustn't fall asleep.

Step 2

When you are comfortable, close your eyes and then consciously relax all your muscles, starting at the top of your head and moving down through your body to the tips of your toes. If you have difficulty in doing this, tell yourself that you becoming more and more relaxed, that you are going deeper...and deeper...and deeper. It is often helpful to imagine yourself going down, in a lift; on an escalator; in warm water; to the bottom of the sea.

Step 3

Breathe through your nose, and listen to your own breathing. As you become more relaxed you will notice your breathing become slower, shallower, and more restful. Notice that at the bottom of each breath (i.e., after breathing out) there is a pause before you begin to breathe again.

Step 4

When you have noticed these pauses, start counting backwards from ten to one. Count thus: breathe out: TEN: breathe in: breathe out: NINE: breathe in: breathe out: EIGHT; etc. Count in this way from ten down to one, then back up from one to ten, down from ten to one, and so on.

Step 5

Stray thoughts may come into your head while you are breathing/counting. Don't worry about this; just let the thought come, don't dwell on it, let it go. Then go back to TEN and start counting again. Don't worry if you never reach ONE, especially in the early days.

Step 6

Continue breathing/counting in this way for 15 to 20 minutes (although 10 minutes may be easier to start with) at least once a day; twice is better. Keep a watch or clock handy, and check if you wish (otherwise keep your eyes closed). When you finish, remain sitting quietly for a few minutes, then stand up slowly.

FOLLOW-UP

This activity is one that should be incorporated into your life style to be of maximum benefit.

Once you have mastered this basic relaxation technique, you might like to carry it a stage further. On relaxation and meditation techniques, *The Relaxation Response* by Herbert Benson (Collins, 1976) and *How to Meditate* by L. LeShan (Sphere, 1978) are still two of the most useful books around. B. Messing's *The Tao of Management* (Wildwood House, 1989) is a nice book which offers short koans to reflect upon and is from a practising chief executive.

On a broader front, Mike Pedler and Tom Boydell's *Managing Yourself* (Fontana, 1985), especially Chapter 6, 'Managing Your

Health', suggests, via lots of exercises and illustrations, that the healthy life is founded on knowing and valuing yourself. Also in terms of living a healthy life, Cary Cooper and Marilyn Davidson's *High Pressure: The Working Lives of Women Managers* (Fontana, 1982) is accessible and relevant for women and men.

Activity 29

Fitness

LEARNING AREA: EMOTIONAL RESILIENCE

There is a steadily growing recognition of the essential link between physical fitness, on the one hand, and mental alertness, high morale, motivation, and general effectiveness, on the other.

In this activity we simply stress the importance of this aspect of self-development, and make one or two suggestions about the sources of further guidance. For example, many local authorities run 'keep fit' programmes; some colleges put on activities specifically designed for managers and businesspeople; there are also many books on the subject.

You should find a regime of regular exercise which suits you—your personality, life style, age, present level of fitness, and so on—and build it into your work and life. This will not only make you feel physically better, it will have a payoff in all areas of your work—particularly where you are in stressful, demanding situations. To be a successful manager, you can't afford not to be fit!

Fashions in fitness come and go, and new books appear all the time which reflect these. There are many simple ways to improve your fitness—one USA study showed that executives who climbed just fifty steps each day reduced their risk of heart disease by almost half. Giving up using lifts, walking two miles each day, going for a swim twice a week, will all make a difference. Just start doing something.

Activity 30
Managing your feelings

LEARNING AREAS: SOCIAL SKILLS: Emotional resilience: Self-knowledge

One of the factors which contribute to emotional resilience is awareness of one's own feelings. This awareness is a requirement for the control and management of feelings. We do not want to overstress the controlling aspect. The manager who always maintains a stiff upper lip, in classical British tradition, is bottling up natural feelings. The manager may not even fully realize this. One day the dam may burst in some uncontrolled way, leading perhaps to a nervous breakdown or psychosomatic illness.

Open expression of feelings is not only beneficial to the individual, but also leads to more open interpersonal relationships. This must be qualified. If there is a strong norm in your organization that open expression of feelings is somehow taboo, your colleagues may be surprised or even shocked to find you breaking this rule.

We express feelings by what we say, but much more significant factors are the way we say it, and non-verbal cues such as facial expression, gesture, and posture.

The main purpose of this activity is to develop awareness of your feelings so that a choice can be made about their expression. Bottling up or free expression are alternative ways of handling feelings, both appropriate in particular situations. If you bottle feelings up, you'll have to express them somehow, somewhere, but the successful manager 'manages' this expression.

The activity is designed to give you practice at becoming aware of, and expressing, your feelings—and at identifying feelings that are being expressed by someone else.

The activity

Steps 1 and 2 of the activity should be done with a partner, although it is possible to do Step 1 on your own, using a tape recorder. If you do so, follow the instructions, record your voice, and listen to a play-back. Even with a partner, you will derive extra benefit from using a tape recorder.

Interpret that word 'partner' liberally—it can be a colleague, spouse, or friend, or even a small group of four or five persons.

Step 1

The first step focuses on the expression of feelings through the *way we speak,* as opposed to *what we say.*

Copy out this list of feelings on to small cards or pieces of paper—one feeling per piece.

Excited	Patronizing
Angry	Depressed
Sarcastic	Bored
Happy	Tired
Affectionate	Enthusiastic
Disliking	Frightened
Threatened	Curious
Superior	Preoccupied
Cautious	Interested

Shuffle the cards/papers, and select one at random. Imagine that you partner has just said or done something that evokes in you the feeling on the card. Get into the mood of that feeling and then say in a way that demonstrates that feeling, the following:

'Well, now, there are lots of implications in this.'

Your partner has to guess what emotion or feeling you are trying to convey. If he or she is wrong, try again.

Take it in turns to express and guess feelings.

Discuss the experience together. Were there some feelings that you found relatively easy or difficult to express? If so, why do you think this was?

Were you surprised at the level of accuracy or inaccuracy of your partner's ability to perceive your emotion? Or at your own ability to judge your partner's? What are the implications of your answers?

Step 2

This step deals with the non-verbal expression of feelings, such as by facial expression, gesture, body posture, etc.

The procedure is the same as in Step 1, except that instead of expressing feelings through the sentence 'Well, now, there are lots of implications in this', you may do so in any way you wish *provided that you do not speak.*

Again, take turns and then discuss.

Step 3

This step moves back into everyday activities. It requires you to examine the feelings you experience from time to time, to identify how you *think* you expressed them, and to check out this belief with other people concerned.

To help with this, use the 'feelings log', Table A30.1. In column 1, write down how you felt on each particular occasion. Then try to think why you felt that way, and note that briefly in column 2.

1	2	3	4	5
Your feelings at a particular time	*What caused these feelings?*	*Did you express your feelings?*	*If not, why not? If so, how did you express them?*	*Check with others. How did they think you were feeling? Why?*

Table A30.1

It is worth looking out for a phenomenon that many managers experience without being aware of it. Having noted how you felt, try to identify *what you were feeling just before*—even though this preliminary feeling may have lasted for a very short time.

When an event triggers off a particular feeling we often find this unacceptable and switch to another emotion. As was mentioned earlier, anger is often preceded by a brief feeling of threat, anger being a defence against that threat. This insight is helpful in controlling behaviour and in responding more productively to situations. So, if you are able to identify short feelings-links, note these down.

In column 3, answer yes or no to the question 'Did you express your feelings?' If your answer is no, try to explain why not in column 4. If the answer is yes, describe in column 4 how you think you expressed them.

Finally, use column 5 to check out with the other people involved in the situation whether or not they correctly perceived your feelings. Ask them what *they* thought you were feeling, and why. Compare this with your own perception of your feelings, and the way in which you did or did not express them.

After a number of entries in the feelings log, look for patterns or repeating themes. Do certain types of events lead to certain feelings? What different causes lead to a particular feeling? Which feelings do you express, which do you not? Why? When do you express feelings? When don't you? To whom do you express them? To whom don't you? Do people sense some of your feelings, but not others? Are some people more accurate in their perception of your feelings than others?

Activity 31
Stability zones

Reaching the limits of 'emotional resilience' is often experienced as loss of control, of ability to cope with the demands made and the changes going on around an individual. Alvin Toffler suggested that we can all cope with an enormous amount of change, pressure, complexity, and confusion, provided that at least one area of our lives or ourselves is relatively stable. This 'stability zone' serves as a mental retreat and anchor which allows us to cope with change and complexity in other areas.

The main kinds of stability zone are related to IDEAS, PLACES, THINGS, PEOPLE, and ORGANIZATIONS. Working out where *your* stability zones are or could be, and planning to cultivate them, may help you develop your capacity to cope with pressures in other areas.

IDEAS may take the form of a deeply felt religious belief, or a strong commitment to a philosophy, political ideology, or cause. It may take the form of a strong interest in an area of professional activity and its underlying theory.

PLACES mean geographical places: large scale (like your country), or small scale (like your street or your office). Places as stability zones are often 'home', where one grew up or has spent considerable time, and which has a comforting familiarity about it.

People whose stability zones are places will always feel a little strange anywhere else and take comfort from the knowledge that they can return to home base. Managerial careers often demand that one becomes cosmopolitan—living away from 'home' and moving on every few years. Some learn to do without a stability zone, others find ways of keeping some geographical roots alive.

THINGS as stability zones take the form of favourite, familiar, comforting possessions. It may be clothes, like that old jacket or pair of shoes, or it may be family heirlooms. It may be items from childhood or the paraphernalia of a hobby. It may be houses (obviously related to PLACES) or books (related to IDEAS). It is often motor cars.

PEOPLE means valued and enduring relationships with others. Very often family will be the source of PEOPLE stability zones, but it may also be long-standing friends and colleagues.

ORGANIZATIONS as stability zones may be the work organization, a professional body or institute, a club, or any other form of organization to which one belongs and with which one 'identifies'.

Stability zones may overlap, for example 'home' has elements of place, people, and things.

One can cope with considerable change and instability in many of these areas at once, provided one has a stable base in at least one. So, for example, the person centred around an idea, belief, or cause may be able to lead a nomadic life with no enduring possessions, getting through organizations and spouses at great speed.

Activity

Work through the following questions, on paper, making notes in answer to them. They are intended to help you think about your stability zones, whether they do and will serve you well, whether you should deliberately cultivate them.

Step 1. What are YOUR stability zones?

Write down your thoughts, think through the five areas of ideas, places, things, people, and organizations. Ask yourself what you would change and what you would not—your car, your organization, your spouse, your possessions, your house.

Step 2. How stable are your stability zones?

Are your basic ideas and beliefs sound? Can you count on staying in your 'places' and on you places staying the same? Do your possessions continue to satisfy? Will they last, or eventually wear out? Can you count on the people you rely on to stay around? Can you count on the organizations you want to belong to wanting you to belong to them?

Step 3. Will your stability zones serve you in the future?

Things change with the passing of time. Objects wear out, houses become too big or too small, children grow up and leave home, organizations and places change, other people have their own lives to lead, ideas are sometimes found wanting or deficient, or reach their limits. Some activities, like sport, become more difficult with age, and everyone retires sometime, unless they drop dead first!

Step 4. Can you influence the existence of your stability zones?

Are the ideas, places, things, people, and organizations that you depend on to any extent under your control?

Step 5. Do you invest enough in you stability zones?

Do you work on developing your ideas, look after and maintain your possessions, care for the people that are important to you?

Step 6. How compatible are your stability zones with your main, particularly your work, activities?

Step 7. Are there any changes you want to make in your stability zones, and how you use and maintain them?

Write yourself an action plan BY WRITING A LETTER TO YOURSELF AS YOU HOPE YOU WILL BE IN SIX MONTHS' TIME.

FOLLOW-UP

Career Anchors by Ed Schein (Pfeiffer & Co., 1993) is helpful for sorting out the important elements and values in your career. *Women's Career Development* by Barbara White, Charles Cox and Cary Cooper (Blackwell, 1992) helps focus on matters which are central to career moves, and those which are not.

Activity 32
Who's the boss?

LEARNING AREAS: PROACTIVITY: Analytical skills: Social skills

Whatever your level of management you probably have the right to be boss of at least one group of other managers who help you to make important decisions.

In complex, interdependent social systems decisions are very rarely ours to take alone. Just as management has long since lost the right to decide unilaterally (without reference to employees) so most of us must consult and communicate to be able to decide on important issues.

Decisions about changes, decisions on problems, decisions about where to go and what to do are all made and often negotiated with those who are most concerned with the particular decision.

But who is really the 'boss' on important decisions that affect your life? It should be you, and you should be able to choose the team to help you make good decisions and not hold you back. Some people will give as well as take from you; others will only take; their impact is largely destructive. The former cause you to grow and strengthen from your interaction with them; the latter weaken you.

This activity offers you an opportunity to select managers, to establish yourself as the boss over them, perhaps even to remove those whose influence is not helpful, or even harmful.

Activity

Step 1

Choose a decision which has to be made—now or in the near future. Don't choose a decision which has already been taken—the more 'live' the issue the better.

The decision should not be a simple choice between clear alternatives, but a complex matter involving others and their feelings and relationships, and affecting a number of areas of your life.

Choosing a new car would not be a very good example to choose; changing your job or moving house would be. It may be one of your life's goals that you want to change, or some aspect of the way you've been living, perhaps a major decision affecting your children—their education, upbringing, or future.

Step 2

Thinking of this decision and using the 'boardroom' diagram (Fig. A32.1), write in the name of the 'managers' who have a say in the making of this decision. Six to twelve is a good number. Put their initials on the chairs round the table.

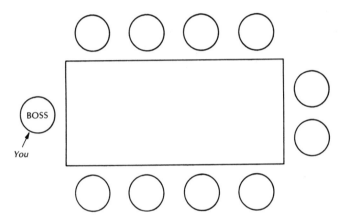

Figure A32.1

Step 3

Next to each of the 'managers' jot down some notes on the advice he or she would give on this decision.

Step 4

Take a good look at this advice. Ask yourself of each manager in turn:

● Whose interest does she or he have at heart in making points, his/hers or yours?
● Is she or he interested in getting a good decision or not?
● How biased is he or she?

Step 5

If you are the boss you take the decisions. You also have a say in who sits on the management team, although you can't remove people just because you don't like them. You need to distinguish between liking a person and concern for a good decision. They have a right to be there even if you don't like their advice.

Take a look at your management team:

(a) Are you really the boss?
(b) Are there any managers who shouldn't be there?
(c) Have you got enough advice of the right kind? Could you use a new manager? Perhaps to replace one of your less useful ones?

FOLLOW-UP

In this activity, we've been talking about putting you in charge of the important decisions that affect your life. From a different angle, if you have a boss who is less than a joy to work with, then Patti Hathaway and Susan Schubert's *Managing Your Boss* (Kogan Page, 1992) offers strategies and techniques for overcoming obstructions and improving collaboration.

Activity 33
Practising change

LEARNING AREAS: PROACTIVITY: Sensitivity to events: Emotional resilience

It is commonplace to talk about the accelerating rate of change in society. More than in any previously recorded age, we have to learn continuously, to cope with and keep up. No one grows old and dies in the world in which he or she was born, and the stresses and demands placed upon us help to account for the explosion of the so-called 'helping professions'. Still, the growth in numbers of teachers, social workers, and medical staff fails to cope with the by-products of change. Voluntary associations find their resources over-stretched and the consumption of anti-depressant drugs speaks for itself.

Change creates problems for management. A large part of management is the efficient administration and deployment of resources via systems, procedures, and routines. This 'determined' part of a manager's job is relatively easy to specify and train for. The other part, the unpredictable 'discretionary' element, can't be programmed. As change increases so does the discretionary portion of a manager's work. Moreover, this is usually the critical portion, the part where the difference between right and wrong decisions can be measured on the balance sheet.

To cope with the job—and to cope with themselves—managers need to become familiar with the effects of change on themselves and on other people. This does not imply that every manager spends all her or his time implementing change. On many occasions we will resist change and seek to minimize its effects. We are, however, responsible for the work of other people and therefore for the effects of change on this work. We need, therefore, to be intimately concerned with the planning of change and the anticipation of its effects.

This activity contains a number of short experiments which call for risk taking to experience and learn about the effects of change. The

207

objective is to practise change on yourself. What you learn as a result of the risks you take and the changes you make will prepare you for changes imposed on you and over which you have no control. It will also prepare you for planning the implementation of change with your staff—you will learn how it feels, what reactions to expect, and how to cope with them.

A word about risk taking. One theory of human change and development suggests that we learn by making *investments* of a modest kind in certain new behaviours. These new behaviours are chosen on the basis of what we know of the world (COGNITIONS) and what we know of ourselves (SENSE OF IDENTITY). We learn from the feedback which we get from these investments—good or bad, pleasant or unpleasant. If we can accept even negative feedback then our cognitions and identity and perceptions are enhanced. Learning always involves risk—we are moving from what we know and are familiar with to what we don't know and are unsure of. The more deep and fundamental the learning, the more risk is involved. Hence 'bad' or 'negative' feedback is important—often more important than 'good' feedback, if only because we often choose to ignore it.

The following activities call for moderate risks from you. They also offer the opportunity of learning about yourself and others. Start with these and if you want to go further, design some of your own risk taking and change situations.

Activities

Experiment 1: Eating a new food

The next time you go to a restaurant, or even the canteen if the menu is varied enough, eat a new dish which you haven't tried before.

Before eating
- What are your expectations about the experience you are about to have?
- It is going to be pleasant or unpleasant, exciting or stressful?
- What are your feelings as you approach the food?

While eating
- Concentrate solely on eating, especially the first mouthful. Chew slowly, don't talk, and don't be distracted from the food.

After eating
- How does this compare with your normal approach to food?
- How much of a risk did you take?
- What did you gain as a result of your investment?

- What did you learn about changing to the unfamiliar?

Experiment 2: Changing your surroundings

Choose a room where you spend a considerable part of your time. If you have an office then this would probably be the best, but if not, try a room at home. The experiment involves rearranging the furniture. You can also take down pictures and remove decorations, or put some up if your room is rather bare.

Before rearranging
- Where else could the major pieces of furniture go?
- What other layout is possible?
- What alterations could be made to the decorations?

Rearranging
- Note carefully where you are putting things in your new arrangement.

After rearranging
- How comfortable do you feel now? (Allow at least a few hours before changing again.)
- What effect does the new layout have on your behaviour? What are you doing differently?
- How do other people react to your new layout? (Try and arrange for as many as possible to view and comment on the change.)
- What have you learned about the effects of physical surroundings?
- What have you learned about change and its effects on behaviour?

If you get something out of this investment, try another layout or rearrangement.

How long is it since you looked at the fixtures and fittings in your behaviour as a manager and considered a spring-clean and re-arrangement?

Experiment 3: Changing your image

Obviously there are many, many ways in which you can do this. For the purpose of this experiment, let's choose three areas of yourself which the outside world has most contact with. These are:

Your style of dress;
Your style of writing;
Your style of greeting.

'Impression management' is a jargon-term for personal public relations. What we suggest here is that you try a few changes in these areas and watch for the results.

Dress

Choose some change or other. Leave your tie off or wear a hat.

Put on a formal suit if you don't usually wear one. Try casual dress if you usually wear a suit. If you wear a suit, embellish the accessories such as shirts, handkerchiefs, brooches. Buy the latest style of suit in a different colour/pattern than usual.

As with all these experiments take careful note of:

- How you feel beforehand;
- How you feel during the introduction and implementation of the change;
- How other people react to you; and
- What you learn about yourself and the effects of change.

Writing style

Change it — somehow. Are you a brief or lengthy memo writer?

Are you conciliatory or aggressive in style? Are you serious or jokey?

Whatever you are or whatever your usual practice, try a change:

- Committee minutes which include some humour make more compelling reading.

Ask yourself the same questions as for 'dress'.

Style of greeting

This is a surprisingly powerful communicator. First, you must recognize your usual routine. Do you greet everyone from floor sweeper to MD effusively and at length or do you sneak to your office avoiding the eyes of everyone?

Select a new approach and try it out. Give your friends a brief and businesslike greeting and go and chat at length with caretakers and cleaners. Buttonhole the MD in the lift and pass the time of day.

Ask yourself the same before, during, and after questions.

For all these experiments give yourself a few minutes of peace and reflection to extract the most from the experience.

Experiment 4: An unpleasant situation

This is the most difficult of the experiments and it is therefore recommended to graduates of the earlier ones.

Choose a situation which you know from experience you will probably not enjoy and would normally avoid.

This might be as simple as digging the garden or cleaning the lounge, or it might be more complex, like spending the whole evening on your own in a bar, or deliberately spending some time with a colleague whom you dislike.

1. List some situations which you find unpleasant and try to avoid.
2. Pick one and deliberately put yourself into it.
3. Record your feelings on paper—before
    —during
    —afterwards.
4. Write a short story changing the outcome of the experience.
5. Identify how much personal responsibility you feel for what happened or did not happen?

FOLLOW-UP

If you enjoyed these experiments and learned something about risk taking and the effects of change, generate some ideas for yourself about things you'd like to change—about yourself, about other people.

Plan how you're going to go about these changes.

Some useful books for practising and managing change have already been listed under activities 15 ('Planning Change') and 16 ('Analysis of Experiences'). In addition to these, Tom Peters' *Liberation Management: Necessary Disorganization for the Nanosecond Nineties* (Macmillan, 1992) is a big, typically high-octane book of examples from all over the world claiming that traditional management methods are being ditched in the face of globalization and fast-forward information technology.

Activity 34
Action planning

LEARNING AREAS: PROACTIVITY: Analytical skills

Action planning is an essential element in the process of learning or accomplishing. With small tasks or problems it is often an automatic process—'from my experience now, the next time I meet this, I'll do it that way'. There is often no need to verbalize or make conscious this process if it is working well.

With bigger problems or tasks automatic systems are rarely adequate. Sometimes, encouraged by their success with small, perhaps mechanical tasks, people will jump into action before they have planned sufficiently.* This may lead them to neglect big issues in the cause of solving many small ones. Another mistake is to think and plan rigorously, but never be quite ready to get down to action.

These problems occur when one is personally faced with a large task. In joint endeavours with other people, action planning is usually a formal requirement built into minutes or agreements—'Samantha Miles will contact Geoff Watts and report back to the next meeting on 15 March'. This form of contract between the people involved, the minutes or record being a negotiated agreement to do specific things at specific times. Where an action plan doesn't exist in written form, joint endeavours only flourish where the action plan is recognized and members take personal responsibility for implementing it.

So here we have the essential elements of an action plan. It consists of setting targets or objectives to accomplish some action or actions; establishing standards of quality or time which act as deadlines *and taking or allocating personal responsibility for these actions*. How often do you say 'Oh, well, I meant to do it but I never got around to it'? In a competitive situation, your customer will go to someone who *does* get around to it. When you write an action plan

*But see Activity 11 'Decision Making' for the case against detailed planning before action.

212

you voluntarily commit yourself to a course of action which you will achieve to a certain standard or by a certain date. It is this *commitment* which is the important aspect of an action plan. Planning is useless without commitment.

Activity

The activity takes you through an action planning sequence with a worked example. You should choose your own example and work it through in parallel.

There are five stages:

1. Setting goals
2. Establishing sub-goals
3. Target dates
4. Resources/methods
5. Standards

You can use a shorter version, stages 1 to 3, if you prefer.

Step 1

Draw up a chart upon which to detail your action plan. It should have five vertical columns (three if you are using the short method) and look something like Table A34.1.

Goals	Sub-goals	Target completion dates	Resources/ methods	Standards

Table A34.1. Action plan chart

Step 2

Choose a problem or task which you are working on or, preferably, about to start working on. Are you the sort of person who makes lists? Lists for shopping; for jobs to do this weekend; for telephone calls to make today? If so, you should have little difficulty in choosing a task. If you don't habitually make lists, try doing one now.

- Suppose you are told to clear your desk in preparation for a top priority job which is coming in a month's time:
  1. List all the things you would have to do in order to get your desk clear by then.
  2. Now choose the *most difficult* task on that list.

Write your tasks in the left-hand column of the Action Plan Chart. The example used here is an appraisal one:

TASK: Appraise the work section.

Step 3

Large tasks have a way of looking impossible, which is why most of us use every opportunity to avoid them. Setting sub-goals involves breaking up the main tasks into manageable proportions. They are often also the means by which the major goal is achieved, so in the case of our worked example:

Major goal: Appraising the work section
Sub-goals: (a) Memo reminding all concerned of annual appraisal.
(b) Interviews with:
Rose Smith;
Maria Correlli;
George Evans;
Helga Martin;
David Salmon.
(c) Complete documentation and circulate for agreement.
(d) Make returns to personnel department.
(e) Make individual action plans for any training needs arising out of appraisal.

Are you managing to work *your* chosen goal into sub-goals? Questions which might throw up sub-goals are:

- 'What are the ways in which I could attain my goal'?
- 'What is involved in this task'?

Fill in these sub-goals in the second column of the Action Plan Chart.

Step 4

Setting target dates is straightforward. Set them for your sub-goals first and then estimate the likely date for your overall goal. You may have a deadline already, in which case you will have to plan sub-goal deadlines to help you reach this.

Fill in target completion dates on your Action Plan Chart. Remember these are your deadlines—failure to achieve them requires explanation—to yourself or to others.

If you're using the short Action Plan, you are now complete. Read the next two steps to see what isn't in your plan.

Step 5

The resources and methods column answers the questions:

'How am I going to tackle this problem?'
'What alternative courses of action are open to me?'
'What assistance do I need and what can I get?'

In our example, resources include:

(a) Appropriate documentation from personnel dept.
(b) Notes on appraisal interviewing from last management course.
(c) Any other useful things in personnel and training, e.g., films, checklists, tips, etc.?
(d) Jack Williamson (source of advice).

Methods include:

(a) Circulating via internal post where appropriate and possible.
(b) Personal interviews (allow $1\frac{1}{2}$ hours for each).

Fill in resources and methods on your Action Plan Chart. In trying to complete this column you may discover you don't have sufficient resources and that you need to get these before proceeding. If so, obtaining these resources then becomes a sub-goal which precedes the others.

Step 6

When you have completed the Action Plan Chart, subject it to critical appraisal. Do this yourself or, perhaps better, get someone who knows about you and the task to do it for you. Examples of the searching questions to ask are:

• 'Is this goal really important for your department?'

1. *Goals*	2. *Sub-goals*	3. *Target completion dates*	4. *Resources/ methods*	5. *Standards*
1. Appraising the work section		31 January		Sub-goal 2: 　1. Develop personal, private, and confidential climate
	1. Memo to all concerned	4 Jan.	*Resources:* 1. Documentation (personnel)	2. End each interview only after:
	2. Interviews: 　Rose Smith 　Maria Correlli 　George Evans 　Helga Martin 　David Salmon	18 Jan. 19 Jan. 20 Jan. 21 Jan. 22 Jan.	2. Appraisal notes (last course) 3. Anything else in personnel, films, etc.? 4. Jack Williamson	(a) got all information 　　(b) I feel I've improved relationship 　　(c) each interviewee has said all; been satisfied or agreed a course of action.
	3. Complete documentation and circulate	22 Jan.	*Methods:*	
	4. Make returns to personnel	29 Jan.	—Internal post —Personal interviews (1½ hrs each)	Sub-goal 3: 　Seek *commitment* rather than mere compliance
	5. Make individual action plans on any identified training needs	say, by 1 March		Sub-goal 4: 　Ensure correctness to avoid return of documents
				Sub-goal 5: 　Action plans to conform to specification

Table A34.2. Completed action plan chart

- 'Will these sub-goals lead to achievement of the main goal?'

By now you have an Action Plan Chart, see Table A34.2.

- 'Can that time target be shortened?'
- 'Will those performance standards tell you how well you're doing?'

FOLLOW-UP

You can draw up an Action Plan Chart for any number of tasks or goals. It will give you a clear picture of what is involved in the completion of any complex task and also supply the discipline and commitment necessary for the completion of that task. This activity is similar to others in this book concerned with planning and analysis. If you have not done so already, try Activity 11 'Decision Making', Activity 12 'Planning and Decision-Making Techniques' or any of several others related to this area.

If you want to study action planning further, most general management books will have something on rational planning and target-setting methods such as Management by Objectives (MbO). References to project planning are given in Activity 26 ('Collaborative Working') and you might also want to think about the time-planning ideas in Activity 3 ('Managing Your Time'). For interesting views on the limits of rationality, you could browse through Gareth Morgan's *Images of Organisations* (Sage, 1986) which shows that linear thinking belongs in the 'organizations as machines' view of the world and that there are many other ways of understanding how things happen.

Activity 35
Imaging

The difference between 'imaging' and 'imagining' is that when we 'image' something we intend that thing to happen or come about. Once when I worked in a part of an organization six miles from the main building, I had to make infrequent trips to the town centre where this main building was located. On one particular day I travelled with a colleague who, after a couple of miles, remarked quietly and seriously that he was 'thinking up a parking space'. As it was his car in which we were travelling and he had been kind enough to offer me a lift, I restricted myself to an uneasy chuckle. However, when we got to the appointed spot, sure enough there was a vacant space. Coincidence? 'It's never failed yet', my colleague said, matter of factly.

There is nothing new about 'the power of positive thinking'. Studies of high-achieving people like athletes, managers, and other performers show how often successful people tend to visualize the results they want in their work and lives. So the idea of bringing about reality through thought has been around a long time. Prayer is perhaps the commonest form of this, while at the other end of the scale of human endeavour we have been known to bring harm to other people, sometimes with the aid of a little effigy and some pinsticking. There is clearly great power here, albeit working in a way which we don't understand. With this great power, of course, comes the possibility of great abuse. Ex-President Nixon was a great believer in 'PMA—Positive Mental Attitude'. Was it this sense of power that corrupted him?

At a more mundane level, we talk about needing leaders or managers with 'vision'. In saying this we are recognizing that development doesn't happen through rational planning and the restructuring of departments, but through first creating a picture of what we want to happen. 'What will it look like?' we ask, and we

218

follow the person with the best picture. 'Imaging' then is the everyday activity of creating a vivid picture of what we want to bring about—at work, in relationships, and in ourselves—'As a man thinketh in his heart, so is he' (Proverbs).

Activity

Step 1

Choose a situation, a relationship or an aspect of yourself that you would like to change or influence. Perhaps you could take something from the activity 'domain mapping' (Chapter 3) which will have left you with a lot of work to do.

Step 2

Now think about this aspect of work, relationship or yourself. Try to build up a picture of how you would like it to look. What would be the best picture you could imagine? Now what do you want it to look like? Visualize the results you want in this situation.

You might find this quite difficult at first. Some people get pictures easily while others don't. If you're having difficulty try:

- writing down every day the qualities and characteristics you'd like to see in that situation. Write a list of these, e.g., 'I want my relationship with Majeed to be more open; more friendly; less "careful"; more fun but also more productive. I want to see us finish the Anshan project. I see us having a drink in the Victoria celebrating our success. I see us picking a new project together— one that will use my ability to organize resources and his confidence and ability to keep going, etc.'
- drawing a picture or making a collage by cutting out images and pictures from magazines and pasting them on a sheet to build up the image of what you want. When you've got the picture, you can focus or meditate on it when you have the chance. In this way, the image you have of what you want will gradually come about, e.g., if I want to change my room, I can try out all sorts of decors, types of furniture, plants, equipment, I can experiment with layout and even ask other people what they think before taking the plunge. I can cut out from this magazine just the sort of desk I want; I can photograph or draw in my existing things that I want to keep, etc.

Step 3

When you have a good picture of what you want to bring about keep thinking about this, bringing it back to mind or taking it out to focus on it from time to time. Gradually over time, without planning in detail, your image of what you want will begin to appear through the working of your intuition in the multitude of everyday decisions that you make and which bring your goals nearer.

Bring the picture back and look at it every day or every few hours.

Step 4

There is another step here for those who lack confidence about achieving their image or who perhaps are put off by the idea that it is 'tempting fate'. In a sense this is true, it is tempting fate in that it is a means of influencing future events. It is difficult, however, to imagine a manager managing without planning, i.e., attempting to influence future events. 'Imaging' is an alternative and perhaps a necessary precursor to planning. It's just a bit unusual in our heavily 'rational' managerial culture, with all its graphs, printouts, and flow charts.

Maintaining an image requires strength and stamina. All too often the vision fades and the magic is lost. One way to sustain yourself is by daily *affirmation*. An affirmation is simply saying (or writing down) to yourself a positive statement about yourself and your image. For example, if I were determined to become less irritable and I had an image of myself as smiling, gentle and relaxed, then I might say 'I, Mike, am becoming more gentle, relaxed and smiling every day'. If you were imaging a more creative, productive office, you could say 'Every day, in every way, this office is getting more creative and more productive'.

Choose a suitable positive affirmation, naming yourself or the people or the situation and say it to yourself every day, preferably out loud, preferably several times, say six. Alternatively, or additionally, you can write down your affirmation. Do this 20 times each day.

(You might feel a bit silly 'affirming yourself'. Perhaps it is a bit silly, but then lots of things in this life are. Remember, being able to be silly at times is an important aspect of creativity and, more importantly, having fun. 'I didn't get where I am today without being able to be silly . . .!')

FOLLOW-UP

Having fun may be one aspect of 'imaging', but the power in this is not to be taken lightly. Use 'imaging' for good ends, not to denigrate people—and constantly question your definition of 'good' in this situation. If you want more information on this idea Vaune

Ainsworth-Land's 'Imaging and Creativity; an integrative perspective' in *Creative Management* (Sage/Open University, 1991) edited by Jane Henry, gives an introduction. Gareth Morgan's view that we 'co-produce' our worlds in a partnership of our own inner ideas and more outer realities is given full rein in *Imaginisation* (Sage, 1993). Further exercises can be found in Mike Pedler and Tom Boydell's *Managing Yourself* (Fontana Paperbacks, 1985).

Activity 36
Accepting other people's ideas

LEARNING AREAS: CREATIVITY: Analytical skills: Self-knowledge

Most of us are all too familiar with occasions when we put forward new ideas—to the boss or to experts from other departments—only to find them blocked or rejected without fair hearing. Two of the activities in this book are designed to help you in such situations: Activity 15 'Planning Change' and Activity 13 'Choosing Solutions with a Chance'.

How often is the boot on the other foot? How often do you, as someone else's boss, or as an expert, reject ideas without a fair hearing? We suspect that this might happen more often than you imagine.

The activity

Look out for occasions on which you turn down other people's ideas. Often these people will be members of staff, but there may sometimes be other managers involved.

Step 1

On each occasion write down a list of as many possible reasons as you can think of as to why you reject an idea. Be open and honest. Write them down without qualification, evaluation, or discussion. Such a list might include:

- The idea is impractical.
- It is too expensive.
- It is administratively inconvenient.
- It challenges your basic beliefs.
- It renders irrelevant, redundant, or null and void the work in which you have already invested time and energy.
- It will cause you a lot of administrative or political headaches.
- It involves risks that you yourself are not prepared to take.
- You just don't like/respect the person putting forward the idea.

- It makes you feel unnecessary, redundant; it devalues your ideas or your role.
- You can't accept that other people in general, or this person in particular, can have better ideas than you.
- It causes you to lose face, to backtrack on previously stated ideas or beliefs.
- You don't want this other person to take credit.

Step 2

Look over the reasons you have given. Challenge them. Cross-examine yourself. Imagine you are a barrister challenging a witness (yourself). For example:

'How do you know it's impracticable? Have you tried it? What happened? Why? Why not?'
'What do you mean, too expensive? What are the detailed costs and benefits? How could it be done cheaper? It's your job to be able to do this, isn't it?'
'Are you sure you are not rejecting this idea because of the person who made it? What would you say if I pointed out that you nearly always reject ideas put forward by this person? Why is this?'

And so on.

This technique of self cross-examination can be very powerful. (It is a particular version of Activity 48 'Conversations with Yourself'.)

Step 3

What you do next is very much dependent on your 'verdict' following self-examination. Having identified some of the *real* reasons why you are blocking/rejecting the idea, you will need to explore these further—with yourself and with the other people concerned. Draw up a list of changes that you will make in response to an idea ('I will try, with the others concerned, to *make* the thing practicable, to *cut* its costs, to *overcome* administrative/political difficulties').

FOLLOW-UP

The most important follow-up is to incorporate this way of responding into your normal everyday managerial behaviour. In this way you will increase the effectiveness of both yourself and your colleagues.

Activity 37
Brainstorming

One of the blocks that gets in the way of creative problem solving is that of making premature judgements. We often think of novel solutions or ideas, but, simply because they are unusual, we reject them immediately as nonsensical, impracticable, too expensive, and so on; the 'yes, but . . .' syndrome.

Another common block is that of narrow vision, or stereotyping. Because we are used to doing things in a certain way, we close our minds to alternatives, so that after a time they just never occur to us.

Brainstorming is a technique designed to overcome these two blocks to creative thinking. It can be done individually or in a group. We will describe first how to brainstorm on your own, and then make one or two points about doing it in a group.

Activity

To get a good idea of the nature of brainstorming, we will use a fairly unimportant problem as an example.

Step 1

Write down the answer to the following question:

'What are paper clips used for?'

Step 2

Unless you are a relatively fluent and innovative thinker, you will almost certainly have written only one or two uses for paper clips. You will almost certainly have said something about 'holding two or more pieces of paper together'.

224

Step 3

Now write down, in five minutes, as many *other possible* uses of paper clips as you can think of. Don't worry how unusual, peculiar, or odd some of these might be. Write them down and keep thinking of more until the five minutes is up.

Step 4

Clearly, there is no right answer, and individual lists will be very different. You will probably have come up with between 10 and 30 possible uses.

Look for the sort of attributes of paper clips that you have used. They have hooking/linking properties (e.g., chains; hooks; use for unlocking a car door through a partly open window); they can be straightened out (use as axles, spindles, spigots); they have sharp ends (for punching small holes, use as a defensive weapon—in an attacker's face or eye; as a cigar cutter, as a cocktail stick); they are flexible (use as binding wire); they conduct electricity (contact maker, fuse, various electrical connections); they are magnetic (use with a magnet, for picking up light ferrous objects from narrow or bent holes). The more attributes you have made use of in your list, the greater the extent to which you have overcome the stereotyping problem. The act of forcing the pace and making a quick list also helps to overcome the premature evaluation blockage. At this stage, there isn't time to think of reservations or 'yes, buts'.

Step 5

Now think of a real problem facing you. Again, without pausing for evaluation, force yourself to list as many possible solutions as you can. Don't at this stage allow yourself to consider all the implications, pros and cons of each solution. Just get a good list—the longer the better.

Step 6

Now is the time for evaluating these possible solutions. Take each in turn, try to remain open-minded about them, consider all the strengths, weaknesses, consequences, requirements, and implications. You might find Activities 15 ('Planning Change'), 13 ('Choosing Solutions with a Chance'), and 34 ('Action Planning') particularly useful here.

FOLLOW-UP

Brainstorming can be used very effectively in groups. The problem is stated and each member shouts out possible solutions, which are written up on a blackboard or, preferably, a flip chart by a member acting as scribe. During this process it is vital that no evaluation takes place. This prohibition applies to such subtle evaluations as laughing, expressions of wonder, amazement, approval, and derision. It is only when ideas are exhausted, and a very full list has been prepared, that careful, considered evaluation should be attempted.

Robert Boostrom's *Developing Creative and Critical Thinking* (NTC, Verulam, 1992) is full of activities for developing clear and imaginative thinking as well as analytical skills. Tudor Rickards' *Creativity and Problem-solving at Work* (Gower, 1990) is another useful book full of ideas.

Activity 38
Approaches to creativity

Many techniques and approaches have been suggested for creative solutions to problems. Some of these are simply ways of kicking yourself into seeing something new, or in regarding something familiar in a new way. Here are a few of them:

Draw the problem: Whether or not it is obviously a visual or spatial problem, try to represent it in pictorial/cartoon form. Be as uninhibited as you can. Then consider possible solutions, or topics related to the problem, and draw them.

Be the problem, or part of it: For example, imagine that you are the troublesome part of a machine, or an object that has got lost or broken, or a message that was misunderstood. Think hard about what it would feel like, what could be done, what would help.

Imagine something completely different: Think of, imagine, anything—an object, an event, an idea. A spider's web, for instance, or a football match, or dissolving. Concentrate on this in relation to the problem at hand. You may spot a link, or get a fresh perspective that will help solve the problem.

Invert the problem: Turn the problem inside out or upside down, or reverse it. For example, instead of putting a product into a package, consider putting a package round a product; instead of protecting employees from an industrial accident, protect the accident from the staff.

Turn the problem into an opportunity: there is a corny saying 'every problem is an opportunity', but it is very often true.

Write a story: Fictionalize the problem and the people concerned with it. You could get a completely new angle on the situation.

227

Activity

> Think of one or more real problems from your work situation. Try each of the approaches on it:
>
> Draw it.
> Be the problem.
> Imagine something completely different.
> Invert the problem.
> Think of the opportunities that could arise from the problem.
> Write the story.
> Then note down possible solutions and useful ideas.
>
> In the light of the ideas you generate, reflect on which of the approaches helped you the most. Think of, and try out, other approaches. You will find it useful, and truly interesting, to carry out what may seem at first a rather silly exercise, but we guarantee that you will come up with new ideas and imaginative/creative solutions.

FOLLOW-UP

> Try some of this book's other activities for developing creativity. Above all, to become truly creative you must let yourself go a little. For some useful books, see those listed under Activity 37 ('Brainstorming') and also Jane Henry's *Creative Management* (Sage/Open University, 1991), a collection of good papers on all aspects of organization creativity. Edward de Bono is an astonishingly prolific writer on this topic. You could try the *Atlas of Management Thinking, Six Thinking Hats* (both Penguin, 1990) and *Six Action Shoes* (Penguin, 1993).

Activity 39
Attribute alternatives

LEARNING AREA: CREATIVITY

We are often unable to think of new ways of doing things simply because we are locked in by constraints imposed by our assumptions about the way things should be done. One way of trying to overcome these constraints is to identify the attributes of the current method, and then generate a list of alternative attributes.

Activity

Step 1

Note down the method or device currently in use, with its main characteristics and attributes.

For example—from the dairy industry. Shortage of milk bottles is forcing us to consider alternative containers.
Current container: bottle.
Attributes: glass; returnable; bottle shape; capacity one pint.

Step 2

Take each of the attributes and consider alternatives to it. At this stage, use the 'Brainstorming' rules (Activity 37). List any alternatives that come to mind and do not attempt to evaluate them. No matter how silly or impractical it seems, list it.

Keeping with our example, we might generate the following alternatives:
Made of: (glass) paper; plastic; wood; aluminium; steel; cardboard; pottery.
Life: (returnable) disposable.
Shape: (bottle) bag; cube; triangle; sphere; hexagon; cylinder; pipe.
Capacity: (1 pint) litre; $\frac{1}{2}$ pint; 100 cc; 10 cc.

Step 3

Examine and evaluate the alternatives. We can consider any combinations, often involving hundreds of permutations. In practice we usually look at some of the more likely combinations.

These must be examined for practicability. Ideas might be logically or technically feasible, but have to be ruled out on grounds of cost, say, or market acceptability. Triangular, waxed paper milk cartons, for instance, have still not really caught on in the UK. Some dairies experimented with milk delivered in one-pint plastic bags—each household being provided with a special jug into which the bag is placed for pouring.

FOLLOW-UP

Keep trying out this exercise with real problems. Remember the important rule: generate as many alternatives as possible, but leave evaluation until later.

For further study on this topic you will find many of the books listed under Activities 37 ('Brainstorming') and 38 ('Approaches to Creativity') of great value.

Activity 40
Coping with complexity

LEARNING AREAS: MENTAL AGILITY: Emotional resilience

Alvin Toffler[1] argued that the stress and disorientation that can be induced by subjecting people to too much change in too short a time is a sickness from which many of us are already suffering.

Coping and adapting to change requires effort in terms of new skills, new knowledge, and emotional stability. We do not here attempt to deal with all of these, but concentrate on that aspect which we call 'mental agility' or 'flexible intelligence'. The concept of intelligence is complex and worrying for most people, who connect it with crude tests which we used to give 11-year-old children.

The intelligence or agility we talk about here is an ability, potential or realized, which everyone has to some extent. It can be improved with practice like any other skill. It is the ability which allows us to do several things at once, switching our minds and resources from one topic to another, making hundreds of decisions as we do so, storing information, recalling it—in short, what all of us do when working in a multi-task situation.

Does a mother's job require the exercise of flexible intelligence? If you doubt it—try this:

Prepare breakfast for four people *at the same time as*:

finding and putting together two lots of dinner money;
cleaning two pairs of shoes;
listening to the news on the radio;
brushing two lots of hair;
talking lovingly to spouse;
talking lovingly to children;
dealing with sundry contingencies
—all in 30 minutes.

How did you get on?

Your work may be just as complex, but you do it instinctively, and therefore without learning how to apply a general skill to new situations. A teacher in a classroom, a supervisor in a machine shop, a manager at a meeting all pursue a number of tasks, observing thousands of stimuli and attending to a few, making many responses and so on—often without much conscious thought about the complexity of the situation.

To help you learn how to respond to new complexity and the contingencies which seem to form an increasing part of every manager's job, try this.

Activity

There are two versions. You are asked to work on certain tasks, thinking consciously about how you are adapting to the skill requirements involved in doing several tasks at once.

Step 1

Make provision for spending a free hour on this activity. Choose six suitable tasks. If you are doing the exercise in the office, tasks might be:

- doing *The Times* crossword;
- writing a paper or notes ready for a meeting;
- planning your work objectives for the next six months;
- telephoning three or four people you need to contact;
- talking to a colleague/your secretary about something which interests him or her;
- preparing statistics/filling in government forms (an Inland Revenue form would be ideal!);
- planning the best new arrangement of furniture in your office;
- reading a behavioural science book on management.

Whenever you are at home, on a train journey, in a hotel, choose tasks that are related to that particular circumstance.

Step 2

(a) Estimate how long each task will take; add up the total time and halve it. (You only ever have half the time you need.)

Now, try to complete all the tasks in that time. Don't do them sequentially, try to do them together, switching from one to the other.

(b) If you find it hard to switch from one task to another, number them 1 to 6; divide your allotted time by a multiple of 6 (12 or 18, say) and, using a dice, change tasks after every one-twelfth or one-eighteenth of your time. For example, if you had allocated 60 minutes, dividing this by 18 will give you approximately 3. Every 3 minutes roll the dice and take up the indicated task. You can switch up to 18 times in a hour, on 6 tasks.

Step 3

Give yourself time to think about the following questions. Take each question in turn and note down your responses.

(a) *What did I actually achieve in terms of completing the tasks?*

(b) *What feelings did I have while doing the tasks?* (Simply jot down as many phrases/adjectives as spring to mind.)

(c) *Have I ever felt like this before? If so, when and where was it? What was the outcome?*

(d) *Could I have been better organized or better prepared?* (If so, how would you go about it next time?)

(e) *Could I increase my ability to deal with multi-task situations?*

If your answer to (e) is 'yes', repeat this experiment in many situations. Remember that the most important thing is to be consciously aware of what you are doing and when you are doing it, and to give yourself time for reflection afterwards. Without this you will miss the learning potential inherent in your own experience of a situation.

FOLLOW-UP

Complexity is a topic in itself—there is even something called Complexity Theory. Biologist Roger Lewin's book *Complexity* (Dent, 1993) critically examines the ideas. More generally in organizations and society, Charles Handy's *The Age of Unreason* (Arrow, 1991) and Peter Drucker's *Post-capitalist Society* (Butterworth-Heinemann, 1993) suggest what may be in store for us.

REFERENCES

1. Toffler, A., *Future Shock*, Pan, 1971.

Activity 41
Quick thinking

In all the research on effective management, the only characteristic found consistently to predict success is some measure of general intelligence.

The nature of managerial work demands the ability to think through complex matters, to think quickly on one's feet, and to switch rapidly from one problem to another.

There is a widely held popular belief that intelligence is an innate human characteristic which cannot be developed through training. This idea is taken from early psychological theories which have long since been questioned and rejected. Current thinking on the question is complicated, but it is clear that the kind of mental abilities that make up intelligence can improve significantly through experience and practice. The following activity is designed to give you practice in thinking quickly on your feet.

Activity

You need ten filing cards or small pieces of paper, and a tape recorder.

Step 1

Write one of the following topics on each of the five cards:

Pay policy
Productivity
Consumerism
Industrial relations
Safety

Step 2

Write one of the following types of audience on each of the remaining five cards:

235

Group of trade union officials
Party of visiting Japanese business people
The sixth form of your local school
Party of American tourists
Group of senior citizens

Shuffle each of the sets of cards separately and put them face downwards so that you do not know what order they are in.

Step 3

Turn on the tape recorder. Pick up the first card on each pile and talk for one minute on the topic revealed, to the audience as turned up from the cards. After a minute, pick up the second topic and audience cards and talk for another minute. Repeat this until you have used all the cards.

Play back the tape to review how well you did in keeping to the topic and relating it to the audience in each instance.

Re-shuffle the cards and repeat the activity. Think up additional topics and types of audience if these become over-familiar.

FOLLOW-UP

Thinking skills come with practice, so the more you can exercise them, the more they will develop.

You should be able to find plenty of opportunities for this in the context of your work. If you want further exercises to work at, try Edward de Bono's *Atlas of Management Thinking* (Penguin, 1990). You can get IQ test practice programs for your computer now, and many management and business bookshops sell practice versions of the Princetown test—the one often used for selection of business school MBA courses.

Activity 42
Developing a helicopter mind

LEARNING AREAS: MENTAL AGILITY: Balanced learning habits: Creativity

An extensive study of managers in one large organization concluded that a quality called 'a helicopter mind' is a key determinant of successful management. 'Helicopter mind' means an ability to think in both concrete and abstract terms, and to move rapidly between the two, linking abstract ideas to specific ideas for action. Managers who think in this way are good at linking theory to practice so that each improves the other.

What determines whether thinking moves 'up' to the abstract, or 'down' to the specific, is the kind of question with which one is faced. In general, 'why?' questions move up, and 'how?' questions move down. You can ask 'how?' and 'why?' about *activities* and *statements of 'fact'*. For example, selecting people for jobs can be analysed this way:

WHY?—To produce enough to meet orders.
↑
WHY?—To get good enough people to work the machines.
↑
TASK—SELECT PEOPLE FOR JOBS.
↓
HOW?—Assess skills needed, test applicants for these.
↓
HOW?—Study existing staff, develop tests to demonstrate skills.

Having answered 'why?' questions it is possible to move down again with 'how?' questions, and develop alternative solutions:

TASK—To produce enough to meet orders.
↓
HOW?—Get more people to work machines OR get faster machines.
↓
HOW?—Offer overtime OR recruit more people.

237

If one starts with a 'statement of fact', one can ask:

WHY is this true?

and

HOW can this be applied?

For example, see Fig. A42.1:

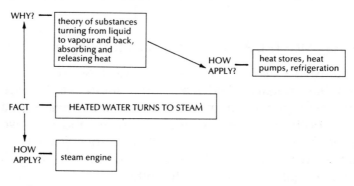

Figure A42.1

Again, asking 'how?' questions after 'why?' questions can generate new alternatives and ideas.

Activity

Practise analysing *activities* and *facts* relevant to your work activities, using both 'how?' and 'why?' questions.

A good way to do this is to write down the activity or fact in the middle of a large blank piece of paper and build answers to 'how?' and 'why?' questions around it. It will look something like Fig. A42.2 overleaf.

In doing the activity, and in your thinking in general, you should aim to think in terms of 'how?' and 'why?' rather than mainly in terms of one or the other.

FOLLOW-UP

You may find it useful to use some of your how/why analyses as the basis for discussion with others who share the same concerns.

Broad reading of things which you may regard as 'academic', 'theoretical', or 'philosophical' may add to your stock of abstract

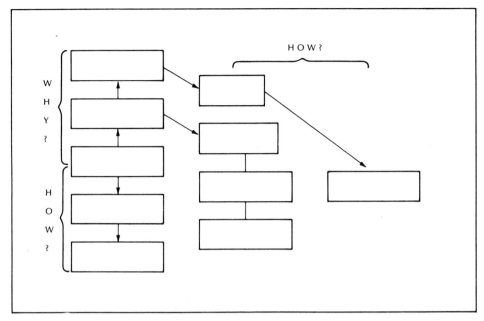

Figure A42.2

ideas that you can relate to the specifics of your work activities. Libraries and educational institutions are good sources of these.

Tony Buzan's *Use Your Head* (BBC, 3rd edn, 1989) which covers his 'mind mapping', is useful for helicoptering, as are other books suggested in Activities 37 ('Brainstorming') and 38 ('Approaches to Creativity').

Activity 43
Managing your dependency

LEARNING AREAS: BALANCED LEARNING HABITS

The theme of this book is *self-development* and that for real learning to occur you must take personal responsibility for your own learning.

In a sense we are urging you to move from:

Dependence—accepting uncritically what teachers and people with formal authority over you may present as the 'right way' to do things

to:

Independence—taking instructions from teachers and authority figures as suggestions which you may try out and evaluate for yourself, adding them to your repertoire of skills and practices if *you* judge them to work.

However, the *independence* philosophy can easily be overdone and lead to a kind of obstinate unwillingness to accept help and guidance from people well qualified to give it. The properly independent person may make extensive use of *mature dependency*— making full use of advice and help from others with genuine expertise and experience. For wisdom to be passed from person to person and generation to generation, so that the benefit of others' past successes and failures can be passed on, mature dependency must play a part.

Activity

Step 1

Make a list of six or so major tasks or activities which you have to perform in your work: preparing budgets, negotiating and bargaining, designing new products or procedures, providing leadership for a team or group, advising others, selling things or ideas, planning operations, interviewing and so on. Write them down in the first column of Table A43.1.

Task/ activity	Are you an expert?	Do you know of an expert?	Do you believe an expert exists?	Or is it an, as yet, unsolved problem?

Table A43.1

Step 2

Taking each of these tasks or activities in turn, go through each of the following questions, stopping when you feel you can answer 'yes' to one of them. Record your answer by putting a tick under the first question to which you can answer 'yes' for each task or activity. There should be only one tick for each task or activity.

(a) In terms of practical ability to carry out this task or activity, do you believe that you are expert at it, in the sense that there is no one else who can do it better than you and that you can reliably deal with it?

(b) If not, is there an expert or source of expertise that you know of who/which does or could provide you with help on this task?

(c) If not, do you believe that somewhere is a procedure, technique, approach, or person which/who can provide a reliable solution to carrying out the task?

(d) If not, presumably you must regard this as one of those tasks or problems for which, at the moment, no known solution exists, and you have as good a chance as anyone else of finding one?

Step 3

Now treat each of your answers as a statement to be *tested*. Consider what *evidence* you have. Are you really fully competent? Can the 'expert' really produce results? Can you track down an expert or authoritative source of knowledge on the problem?

It will be particularly useful if you show your conclusions to someone else who is familiar with the same tasks and problems, and who will give you an honest opinion about your conclusions.

FOLLOW-UP

You may find it useful to follow up this exercise with some exploration into what expertise there is around to deal with problems which you are facing. There may be sources within your own organization, in libraries, or in educational institutions in your area, for instance.

Consider whether your personality leads you to believe in, seek out, and rely on experts, or whether you tend to go it alone; and whether this helps or hinders you.

Consider, and discuss with colleagues, whether your organization has a culture of relying on experts or finding its own solutions, and whether this is functional or not.

Activity 44

Understanding your learning processes

LEARNING AREAS: BALANCED LEARNING HABITS: Self-knowledge: Sensitivity to events

There are five stages to learning a new skill or ability:

- Feeling a need for new behaviour and becoming aware of inadequacies in the way you do things.
- Identifying the behaviours involved in a new skill or activity.
- Practising these behaviours.
- Seeking and getting feedback on your performance.
- Integrating the behaviours into your repertoire of skills and abilities.

This activity aims to get you thinking about how you acquired your existing repertoire of skills and abilities. Being able to learn from everyday experience is a skill in itself, and the need for this ability grows daily. Until recently, the most popular theories about learning were those which suggested that much of our adult behaviour was learned in the first five years of life. More recently, we have become aware of the need and potential for continuing education, beyond the formal years of schooling. Lifelong education is especially vital for managers whose responsibilities demand that they cope with and manage accelerating change.

Learning to learn is therefore an activity on which it is worth spending time. It will help you ultimately with everything you need or want to learn in the future.

In this activity, you are asked to look at some examples of where you have been successful as a manager; what skills or abilities helped you to be successful; and how you acquired those skills.

Activity

Step 1

Think of two incidents in the past year where you have been successful as a manager. These are 'high spots' or 'peak experiences' — the sort of thing you would talk about in a promotion interview to demonstrate your strengths. Now describe these events — what actually happened and what did you do exactly? Write these down and be as *specific* as you can.

INCIDENT 1

What happened?

What did you do?

INCIDENT 2

What happened?

What did you do?

	Skill/ability	Where did I learn it from?	How did I learn it?
1.			
2.			
3.			
4.			
5.			
6.			

Table A44.1

Step 2

Looking at what you did in these two cases, what were the key *skills* and *qualities* within yourself that enabled you to do what you did and to achieve a successful outcome? Write these down in column 1 of Table A44.1. Then answer these two questions:

(a) *Where* did I learn it from?

- from the boss?
- from school?
- from doing the job?

- from a book?
- from my colleagues? etc.

You will also find it useful to recall over what period of time and at what stage in your life this skill/ability was learned. You can do this by remembering the latest time when you are sure you *did not* have the skill/ability and the earliest time you *did*.

(b) *How* did I learn it, i.e., what process was involved?

- by being told something?
- by imitating somebody?
- by puzzling it out for myself?
- by accident or on purpose?
- through emotional or intellectual channels? etc.

Step 3

Take a blank sheet of paper and write down all the insights you have had so far about *how* you learn. Use the data generated in Steps 1 and 2. When you have got down as much as you can, consider the following questions about your learning processes. Write down any additional insights you get as a result of answering these questions.

(a) How well do the five stages of learning a new skill or ability fit with your experience of your learning?
(b) Do you learn different things in different ways; if so, what things and in what ways?
(c) Think about other people you know well and how they learn. Are there any processes which you do not use?
(d) Does receiving 'inputs'—being told or shown something— figure in your learning processes?
(e) Does imitating other people, or learning by observing the success and failures of their actions, figure in your learning processes?
(f) What is the place of emotion and feelings in your learning? Is learning painful, pleasant, or what?

Step 4

This will test your understanding of how you learn and also make some demands on your creativity and ingenuity. *You need a clear 30 minutes for this step:*

(a) Choose a personal skill or ability which you would like to improve.
(b) Spend *10 minutes* designing a very small learning event for yourself. It should last not more than 10 minutes. Use any

resources you see around you and all the insights gained from analysing your past learning experiences. Be prepared to be adventurous, creative, and open to the experience which will happen.

(c) Do the learning exercise. Keep to the 10 minutes.

(d) Evaluate the experience for 10 minutes:

- Did it work?
- Why did it work (or not work)?
- What increased understandings do you have about your learning processes?

FOLLOW-UP

Learning how to learn is not easy, but it is, perhaps, the ultimate management skill. Understanding your learning processes is one way to improve your ability to learn. Work on this, and the rest of the managerial skills and abilities come much more easily.

If you prefer to reflect and think a little before trying more activities in the light of what you have learned about your own learning processes, do so; you are the director of your own learning programme.

One of the best books on how adults learn is David Kolb's *Experimental Learning* (Prentice-Hall, 1985). Building on this, Peter Honey and Alan Mumford's *The Opportunist Learner* (Peter Honey, 1990) and the *Manual of Learning Styles* (Peter Honey, 3rd edn, 1992) offer analysis of your learning style and useful ways of thinking about better learning.

Everybody learns more and more easily in a Learning Company. Mike Pedler, Tom Boydell and John Burgoyne's *The Learning Company: A Strategy for Sustainable Development* (McGraw-Hill, 1991) contains ideas on what a Learning Company is and 101 'Glimpses'. Peter Senge's *The Fifth Discipline: The Art and Practice of the Learning Organisation* (Doubleday Currency, 1990) is full of interesting material on learning disciplines, disabilities and systems thinking.

Activity 45
Study skills

LEARNING AREAS: BALANCED LEARNING HABITS: Professional knowledge:
Self-knowledge

We often say 'she is very clever' or 'he is very bright' about someone who is obviously well educated or highly qualified, implying that they are more able than the rest of us. Unfortunately, professional qualifications are often taken as a measure of a person's worth, and people of ability are handicapped by the lack of them. Intelligence or basic ability is only part of the game of obtaining professional qualifications; opportunity and chance often form as large a part. Another aspect is application—a most important aspect of which is skill at studying. Study skills are different from the other components of academic success because you are not born with them and you do not acquire them by chance. You have to learn them.

Study skills are important whether you are professionally qualified or not. They are important to all managers and they contribute to that illusive skill of being able to learn from one's own experience. Qualified managers may well have picked up study skills in the process of becoming qualified. Those who are unqualified or underqualified may find they are lacking a skill which can be remedied with time and effort.

Before going further, it is necessary to do some diagnosing to discover your own skills and deficiencies in this area.

Activity

We do not have the space here to make you proficient in all study skills, but it is possible to do some diagnosis and point you in the right direction. Complete Questionnaire 1 (Table A45.1) to get an estimate of your overall study skill level.

To evaluate yourself simply add up the circled numbers. The *very best* way to use this questionnaire is to complete it *prior* to some period of study, and then after to see if you feel you have made an improvement.

248

	This is a big problem for me	This is something of a problem for me	This is not a problem for me
For each question, circle one number—1, 2, or 3—in the columns at the right.			
Here are some tasks which have to be achieved for successful study.			
'How difficult is it for you to . . .			
1. . . . decide on a suitable *place* for studying?	3	2	1
2. . . . decide *when* to study, or for *how long?*	3	2	1
3. . . . choose your goal, i.e., precisely what you want to learn?	3	2	1
4. . . . decide *how* to achieve your goal, i.e., what study activities to perform?	3	2	1
5. . . . obtain or reach people, books, and other *resources?*	3	2	1
6. . . . deal with *lack of desire* for achieving your goal, once set?	3	2	1
7. . . . deal with *dislike of activities* necessary to reach your goal, e.g., you want to learn Spanish but you hate reading?	3	2	1
8. . . . cope with *doubts* about success?	3	2	1
9. . . . *estimate level of knowledge or skill*—start and finish and also during study to determine progress?	3	2	1
10. . . . deal with *difficulty in understanding* some part or through lack of fundamental knowledge at some stage?	3	2	1
11. . . . be able to *concentrate?*	3	2	1
12. . . . be able to *remember?*	3	2	1
13. . . . be able to *apply* knowledge gained to real life situations?	3	2	1
14. . . . deal with *frustration* arising from speed of learning; material containing opinions rather than clear-cut 'facts'?	3	2	1
15. . . . be able to overcome laziness or inertia despite interest?	3	2	1
16. . . . find fellow learners for mutual stimulation and companionship?'	3	2	1

Table A45.1. Questionnaire 1: study tasks

For each question circle
one number—1, 2, or 3—in the columns
at the right.

Here are some skills involved in
successful study.

'Do you . . .

	Rarely	Sometimes	Usually
1. . . . decide in advance *what* you are going to study and *where?*	1	2	3
2. . . . set yourself goals and sub-goals? e.g., I will read this book between now and then; 30 pages here, etc.	1	2	3
3. . . . meet your deadlines—especially with regard to written work, reports, etc.?	1	2	3
4. . . . read fast enough to read all the books you need to read on any given matter?	1	2	3
5. . . . skim or scan through books using contents pages and indexes, before deciding what to read?	1	2	3
6. . . . consciously read for a purpose, i.e., to gain specific material and not just to 'get everything'?	1	2	3
7. . . . find it possible to concentrate when listening to lectures or talks?	1	2	3
8. . . . take notes when listening to talks or lectures?	1	2	3
9. . . . know how to use library systems to find the books or information you need?	1	2	3
10. . . . write key notes, i.e., headings and sub-headings rather than continuous prose?	1	2	3
11. . . . feel at ease drawing up reports or writing papers?	1	2	3
12. . . . express yourself well in writing?'	1	2	3

Table A45.2. Questionnaire 2: study skills

The measurement which matters is one which matches you against yourself and not against some mythical standard.

However . . .

- if you scored less than *20* you have few study problems (at least as revealed by this questionnaire).
- if you scored between *20 and 30* you do have quite a few difficulties. Spending time on them will benefit you.

- if you scored over *30*, your innate ability is probably being held back through an inability to study.

BUT don't take too much notice of these notional numbers—this questionnaire is only as valid as *you* think it is. Go back through the questionnaire and look at the questions where you circled 3. Then study the ones where you circled 2. What does this add up to in terms of difficulty?

Answers will vary widely with individuals—you must puzzle out what yours mean. For example, an inability to concentrate or to maintain motivation (both very common study problems), may be caused by a huge variety of things. There may be a very simple reason, such as working in a noisy or unsuitable environment; or it may be exceedingly complex. Lack of concentration is a frequent result of emotional upset, and lack of motivation may stem from a deep-seated fear of failure, perhaps developed in childhood. We are not suggesting psychoanalysis as a means of interpreting your questionnaire answers—merely pointing out the wide variety of interpretations possible. You will certainly find it helpful to talk to someone whom you find supportive—preferably someone who has had some counselling experience—perhaps in the Personnel Department?

The sorts of solutions you might come to are:

- Set yourself a STUDY Diary, giving specific periods on given days of the week for study. (Questions 2; 6; 7; 11?; 15?)

- Find your sort of place to study (this may be combined with time). (Questions 1; 2; 5; 15?; 16)

- Establish a self-testing procedure. (Questions 6; 8; 9)

- Establish a rigorous PRACTICE ROUTINE. (Questions 11; 12; 7?; 6?)

- Join a suitable evening class. (Questions 4; 5; 9; 10; 15?; 16)

- Consult an expert or tutor. (Questions 4; 5; 9; 10)

- Set yourself a detailed ACTION PLAN. (Questions 3; 4; 5; 9)

- Get a supportive or sympathetic ally to talk to from time to time—to bounce ideas off; to counsel; to encourage; to discipline, etc. (All questions)

Remember, these are only a few of the possible solutions.

So far we have been talking about overall study tasks—the problems that have to be overcome when studying—usually alone and without a tutor. It is now time to move on to the specific skills involved in studying—reading, writing, and so on. Answer Questionnaire 2 (Table A45.2).

This second questionnaire focuses on several key areas of study skill:

- organizing yourself and your time;
- reading;
- listening to talks or lectures;
- note taking;
- writing.

Obviously you will be helped a great deal in learning what you want to learn if you develop skills in these areas. In the questionnaire you should aim to be consistently circling 3s—if you have several 1s then these are weak areas for you. This is particularly so if you have two or three 1s in any one area, for example, questions 1, 2, and 3 all concern organization.

Study skills take time and purposeful practice to master. If this exercise has helped you to pinpoint or identify particular problems, you can begin to work on these by following up some of the suggestions below.

FOLLOW-UP

Tony Buzan's *Use Your Head* (BBC Books, 3rd edn, 1989) uses mind-mapping to look at note taking, memorizing and developing ideas. *The Good Study Guide* by Andrew Northedge (Open University, 1990) covers ways of studying, essay writing and preparing for exams.

Activity 46
How do you learn?

LEARNING AREAS: BALANCED LEARNING HABITS: Self-knowledge: Sensitivity to events

You may have already completed Activities 44 'Understanding Your Learning Processes' and 45 'Study Skills' which helped you assess how proficient you are at the study skills. This activity is closely related to both the others, but concentrates on the key experiences by which you have learned and do learn those things you need to learn. It increases your ability to learn how to learn, which is a major goal of this book.

In adults, learning takes place usually as a result of existing behaviour being seen by the learner as inadequate in the light of various experiences or things that happen. If the learner is open and willing to learn, examination of these experiences will provide clues as to how existing behaviour can be modified. Adults very rarely learn completely new behaviour—we have so much accumulated experience, some part of which will usually have a bearing on the problem at hand. Often this past experience gets in the way of learning new things: 'I have 10 years' experience of interviewing, why should I go on a course?' Unexamined happenings in life are not experiences— merely things which happened and passed by without impact. Experience is something we reflect upon and which causes us to modify, often in small ways, our perception of situations and the way be behave in them.

This process—which we call the significant learning process—looks something like Fig. A46.1.

Activity

Each of us is a unique blend of inherited characteristics modified over time by all sorts of experiences—some pleasant, many unpleasant. It is often the painful experiences that teach us so much.

253

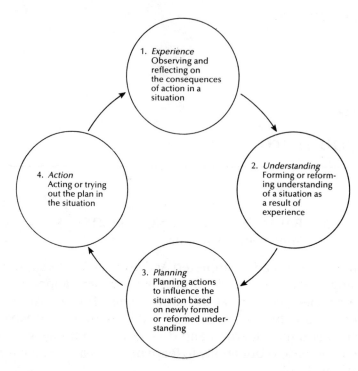

Figure A46.1

To do this activity you need to re-live some of those past experiences. We're going to analyse them to find out just what features made them so important for you.

Step 1

Think of the key learning experiences in your life—the experiences which you feel led to significant changes in your behaviour. They can be short or long experiences, but they must be followed by a discernible change in the way you behaved. Jot down now a title or phrase to label all the experiences which come to mind.

Here's a sample list:

- going to school for the first time
- first love affair
- broken leg
- university degree

Step 2

Take a piece of paper and draw horizontal lines across to divide it into eight equal parts. Use one sheet for each experience and label each sheet. In the eight parts answer the following questions:

1. *What happened?*

2. *What started it?*

3. *What did you learn?*

4. *What words describe how you felt while it was happening?*

5. *Who else was involved?*

6. *Did they help or hinder your learning? How?*

7. *How would you describe the learning process?*

8. *What were the key characteristics of this event—as compared with others in your life when you didn't learn as much?*

Step 3

(a) Look back through your learning experience sheets and seek out commonalities—commonalities in all senses—in how things started; in how you felt; in who was involved, etc.

Write these down.

Can you discern any patterns in your key learning experiences?

(b) Look back through your learning experience sheets and make two lists—one of factors which helped you to learn and one of factors which hindered your learning:

Factors assisting learning	*Factors hindering learning*
(i)	(i)
(ii)	(ii)
(iii)	(iii)
(iv)	(iv)
(v)	(v)
(vi)	(vi)

You should now have an enhanced view of the key learning experiences which have equipped you with the skills and abilities which you possess today. In particular you should know more about patterns in your key learning experiences and what helped and hindered your learning. If you managed to re-live some really painful experiences then you probably drew a good deal of insight out of them. Above all, the activity should help you with *introspection*—a much underrated learning skill which allows you to extract the lessons from your own experience.

FOLLOW-UP

This activity is closely linked with Activities 44 ('Understanding Your Learning Processes') and 45 ('Study Skills') which form a group around the learning theme. The books listed under these previous two activities are also relevant here.

Activity 47
Mind your language

LEARNING AREAS: SELF-KNOWLEDGE: Social skills; Situational facts

> Take care of the sense and the sounds will take care of themselves. (The Duchess in *Alice in Wonderland*)

Some people complain about the difficulty of pronouncing 'Ms'. 'There's no vowel', they protest, 'it sounds awkward'. Funny, saying 'Mr' never seems to cause a problem. While there is a single unrevealing title for men, for women we have three alternatives. Perhaps in a few years these elaborate contortions will subside and people will find that they can pronounce Ms after all, and women will be more comfortable using it as a prefix, without worrying about misinterpretations or assumptions being made about them.

Not long ago a woman in a managerial position was usually referred to as a manageress. Today the word manager is much more likely to be used for male and female alike, except in certain areas of retailing, hotels and catering. In 1600 Margaret Hughes, in the role of Desdemona, became the first woman to perform on a public stage in England. She was then known as an 'actor'—a term used at that time for both men and women. From around 1700 the term 'actress' became the norm. More recently, the pendulum has swung again and 'actor', like 'manager', is used generically.

As Jane Mills points out in her *Womanwords:*

> At first glance, the actor/actress distinction might seem as valid and necessary as the female/male distinction. But *actor* is the generic term and it is the one used by, for instance, their trade union ... and by theatres ..... Miller and Swift apply this formula: 'if the group as a whole is called A, and some of its members are called As and others Bs, the Bs cannot be full-fledged'.

The words we use affect our working relationships. Most of us draw on a lumber-room of descriptive terms without thinking about their origins or the associations they have for others. While trying to avoid the traps of 'PC' (Political Correctness) it is time that the language of the workplace reflected equality in terms of gender, race, age, religion and all the other differences among us. To do this we need to change or eliminate those words which are:

- too narrow in their application;
- indicative of bias;
- offensive to any of our colleagues; or
- simply outdated.

The aim of this activity is to make sure that we don't say or do anything which encourages discrimination on grounds of race, colour, creed, gender, sexual orientation and so on.

Although most of the examples in 'Mind Your Language' are to do with gender, we are talking about all differences between people and how these can either enrich or divide. We need to be especially watchful whenever minorities of any kind are involved. We have all experienced being in the minority—even if relatively trivially such as being young at an older persons' gathering or middle-aged at a teenage party—and the effects on us can be quite disabling. Whether we are welcomed or looked after becomes extremely important—much more so than if we were with 'our own'. And this is not just about avoiding discrimination. The emphasis which some companies place on the importance of diversity and differences in the workforce shows how vital it is today to make the most of the people who make up the organization and all their diverse gifts. We tend to be happiest and most productive where we are welcomed and feel at home.

Does your organization make everyone feel at home?

The Activity

Step 1. Old words; new words

Here is a list of terms in common use in organizations. For each one see if you can think of a better alternative:

Old Term   *Alternative*

1. Manpower planning
2. John Smith and his wife Elsie
3. Male nurse
4. Steeplejack
5. Mankind

6. Headmaster
7. Girls (of women employees)
8. Workmanlike
9. Gentleman's agreement

Testing your alternatives is simple — *could you use that description for every single person in your organization?*

You will find some suggested alternatives at the end of the Follow-Up section of this activity. See if you can extend the list above. Try to add at least another five, from various contexts.

Step 2. Terms of endearment, words of abuse

Start listening to the words you and your colleagues use. Do a bit of research and keep a diary for the next couple of weeks. You could use a grading system such as (+) for the expressions you are comfortable with, (−) for those which make you uncomfortable and (?) for those you're not sure about. Here are some research opportunities and pointers:

1. When you are greeting or being greeted by a colleague (*love, pet, mate, friend*).

What words do you use and what are used to you?

2. When you are praising or being praised (*good girl, well done lad, good man, clever girl*).

What words do you use and what are used to you?

3. When someone you or others admire is being described (*so-and-so is dynamic, a winner, decisive, a good sport, easy-going, doesn't suffer fools*).

Look out for differences in how men and women may be described, and the kind of gestures that tend to go with certain terms.

4. When someone is being put down (*a wimp, a wally, a dipstick, scatty, gossip, hard-faced*).

What (if any) differences are there in how you speak to a man or a woman when you are angry? Are different words used? Is different body language used?

FOLLOW-UP

The best way to find out what is acceptable to others and to help them to belong is by beginning a dialogue about this with the people around you.

You could ask others to record their observations and compare notes with you. You could look at company documentation to see if it is free of bias and stereotypes. Does the language used include everyone? Does it offend or exclude certain people? Do your switchboard operators or reception staff treat all callers alike? A bit of asking around might have interesting results.

There are some very real difficulties in this aspect of our relationships. It is not just a question of 'cleaning up our act', but often of acting to change attitudes which have evolved and persisted over many years. In encouraging you to start exploring and acting in this area, we do not want to suggest that it is without risk. But we have found that some of our own most profound learning about ourselves has come from exploring and understanding differences; and that some of our best efforts and greatest joys have come in collaborative working with people who are very different from us.

If in doubt you can ask people how they want to be called or introduced. Does your colleague who can't see want to be referred to as 'visually impaired' or 'blind', or does she or he want the issue to be ignored? Does the person whose parents were from Pakistan but who was born and raised in Surrey want to be referred to as 'Asian', 'Pakistani', 'black British', 'English', or just by his or her name? They will probably have thought about these things more than we have and, if the request is an honest one and stems from your own concerns, you can save yourself and others a lot of trouble by asking questions rather than making assumptions.

Jane Mills' *Womanwords* (Virago, 1991) is both learned and good fun. The introduction is very good on the connection between language and social change. Casey Miller and Kate Swift's *The Handbook of Non-sexist Writing* (Women's Press, 1989) is an excellent guide, again with lots of amusement to be had — such as the title of a research report: 'Development of the Uterus in Rats, Guinea Pigs and Men'. The book is full of examples and has a glossary of suggested terms. Finally, the *Equality Style Guide*, from the National Union of Journalists' Equality Council (Acorn House, 314/320 Grays Inn Road, London WC1) contains useful advice for writers.

Step 1. Old words; new words

Some possible alternative words
1. Personnel planning; staff planning 2. Elsie and John Smith 3. Nurse 4. ? 5. Humankind 6. Headteacher 7. Women 8. Skilful; effective 9. Unwritten agreement.

Activity 48

Conversations with yourself

LEARNING AREAS: SELF-KNOWLEDGE: Creativity

Talking to yourself—according to a schoolroom joke—is a sign of madness. Art historians will tell you that madness and creativity are closely linked and that what was sometimes described as lunacy we would now call non-conformity or even genius. Each of us has observed abnormality in famous people—it is often this deviation from the norm which makes them creative and famous. There are clear links here with Liam Hudson's concept of 'divergent' as opposed to 'convergent' thinking[1] and de Bono's vertical and lateral thinking.[2]

Hopefully this book will not drive you mad, but a certain amount of experimentation and playfulness is necessary for creativity.

The following activity is very simple and straightforward. It is also very powerful. You'll need a tape recorder, a private room, and at least 30 minutes of uninterrupted time.

Step 1

Go into the room, lock the door, switch on the tape recorder and begin speaking to *yourself*. Do not address any audience or person, real or imaginary. Speak to yourself.

You will find this quite difficult and you may need several starts before you get into it. If you have any doubts, play back what you've said and check whether you are *really speaking to yourself*.

Step 2

When you have mastered talking to yourself you can start on any specific problem or difficult situation facing you. Keep talking until you have said everything you wish to say about this problem.

Step 3

> Play back the tape. Listen until you are satisfied that you understand yourself.

Step 4

> Wipe off the tape before leaving the room—whether you achieved Steps 2 and 3 in their entirety or not. *This is extremely important.*

Step 5

> Repeat Steps 1 to 4 periodically as a means of getting in touch with the problem.
>
> The theory is that whenever we speak, we speak to an audience. We always try to impress or achieve a specific effect upon another or others. We rarely, if ever, speak to ourselves to find out *what we really think.*
>
> Creativity seems to be only partly a conscious process. There is only so much that can be done by conscious effort. Often that 'aha!' or 'eureka!' experience comes after we have slept on or dropped a problem to think about something else. The assumption is that our unconscious mind worked somehow on the original problem and emerged with a solution or breakthrough.
>
> This activity is a formal way of 'thinking aloud'—a more respectable occupation than talking to yourself!
>
> Try it—it may break that block you've been struggling with for so long.

FOLLOW UP

> The books suggested in Activities ('Brainstorming') and ('Approaches to Creativity') offer all sorts of ways forward in developing your thinking and creativity.

REFERENCES

1. Hudson, L., *Contrary Imaginations*, Penguin, 1967.
2. de Bono, E., *The Use of Lateral Thinking*, Penguin, 1990.

Activity 49

Backwards review

LEARNING AREAS: SELF KNOWLEDGE: Sensitivity to events

The ancient dictum 'Know Thyself' is as applicable to today's managers as it was to the old sages who coined it. To know myself—how I act and behave; what my strengths, weaknesses and learning needs are; what motivates and excites me; what scares and dismays me; the effects I have on others and the effects different people have on me; whether I am ambitious or easy-going, etc.—is an important part of being able to manage myself and other people.

When we're going out, or going into an important meeting, we may check how we look—by glancing in the mirror. Finding out about ourselves requires this sort of information, this reflection from something—or someone—acting as a mirror. 'Backwards Review' is a reflective exercise which helps us create a mirror for ourselves. As an exercise it is very simple and quite profound. It takes practice to develop the skill.

Activity

Step 1

This is a simple and basic exercise for becoming more aware of yourself and the situation you are involved in. You can do it at any time, but it seems more appropriate, as it is a reviewing process, to do it at the end of any given episode. You can do this after an important meeting, at the end of three weeks' holiday, or at the end of the year. Because it takes practice to develop this skill, and because it is a very useful and fundamental way of developing awareness and consciousness, it is a good idea to start doing it at the end of each day, just before you go to sleep.

Step 2

First find a quiet place to sit and do the exercise. You can do it lying down—and some people say it's a good cure for insomnia—but that's not the purpose we have in mind here. Anyway, find a place for yourself and one free from interruption and distraction.

Step 3

Now begin to go through the events of the day (or meeting, week, month, etc.) in your imagination. Work *backwards*, starting with the most recent happenings. Try to recall what happened in each event or episode—what did you do? What were you thinking at the time? What feelings were you having? What did you actually want to do at that time and what did you actually do? What were other people doing and what were their thoughts, feelings and wishes?

(As you can see, this 'simple' exercise is quite a task! Do not give up.)

Try to picture, to visualize, what happened. Some people find it easy to bring back pictures in their minds, but others find it hard. Take each episode in turn going slowly backwards, bringing the picture of it into your mind. What did you do? What were others doing? How did you feel? What were your thoughts? . . . and so on.

Step 4

Keep going as slowly as you like until you get to the end—or should that be the beginning?—of the day (or meeting, week, etc.). At first you will find this a bit strange and difficult, so don't be discouraged if you only get a few episodes or hours back. To practise, at the end of each day you can just start with the first hour or two, and gradually extend the time. When you have developed this skill, you will, as a result, have become much more conscious of yourself and your actions, thoughts and feelings, and also have gained some insights into those of other people. You will see more clearly what effects your actions, thoughts and feelings have upon others and how theirs affect you. You will have become more aware in the process of developing a skill which you can use whenever you need it; perhaps especially when your mind feels dull or you need to be extra vigilant.

FOLLOW-UP

Basically, you follow up this activity by taking lots of practice. If you like the exercise and want to explore the notion of 'managing yourself', you can try Mike Pedler and Tom Boydell's *Managing Yourself* (Fontana Paperbacks, 1985).